Love Through Me

Stories from a Missionary Heart

Natalie Ryan

Hearts In Action, Inc. ♡ **Hopkinton, Rhode Island**

Publisher:

Hearts In Action, Inc.
P.O. Box 164, Hopkinton, RI 02833
Telephone: 860-834-1040

Cover Design by Ben Olson

Printed in the United States of America

DEDICATION

For you, Lord, may it all be for your Glory.

For Dr. Brian Quilliam

Enjoy!

Natalie Ryan

CONTENTS

FOREWORD

"LOVE THROUGH ME"... for Christ Followers, it is the cry of our hearts. Surprising as it seems, God chooses all who would follow after him to be the face of His eternal love displayed to a broken and needy world. The plea, captured in the title of Natalie's book, puts in words the passion found in her heart. It is a phenomenon I have witnessed thousands of times over.

From my "front-row-seat," I've observed anxious pilgrims journey to the most impoverished people on our planet only to have their hearts ambushed and made ready for more of Jesus. Read it carefully and see how this godly process becomes apparent through the experiences of the author. Read it prayerfully and see Natalie's experience multiplied in your life.

Stan Horrell, U.S. Director, Mission Discovery

ACKNOWLEDGMENTS

I first want to thank my wonderful husband, Kevin. Without you my life would be incomplete. You are the love of my life, my best friend, and partner. You truly do "shine like the moon." You encourage and challenge me to be all He created me to be. For that I am eternally grateful.

To Justin, our oldest son and the administrative help for Hearts In Action; to John, our youngest, and our interpreter while we were in Guatemala; and to Jeremy, our middle son—I pray you know how much I love you.

Thanks to my beautiful niece, Melissa, who read and re-read parts of this book and offered excellent advice. (Maybe someday we can collaborate on another!) Love you!

Special thanks to Pastor Stan. I was truly blessed to work with you in Haiti. I can only hope it won't be the last time we work together. I've never known anyone who can say so much, impart so much wisdom, with his silence.

Thanks also to Miriam Frederick. Your life exemplifies self-less living, undying strength, and a most faithful advocate for the precious children of Haiti. Thank you for your example.

To Diane Castillo and Claudia Gere for reaching out to me to bring this project to fruition. Thank you for partnering with me, for listening to my concerns, and even not listening if and when it was best for the book! This would never have made it to print without your teamwork and dedication.

To all those who've supported Hearts In Action in prayer, financially, and made this ministry possible.

Finally, a tremendous thank you to all my friends and family. Your love and support mean so much to me.

PREFACE

Did you ever hear a missionary speak and think, "How wonderful! He (or she) is doing such incredible work for God!" and then quickly follow it with "I could never do that"? That's exactly how I felt for over twenty years—until the Lord's perfect timing for me had come.

A little more than eight years ago I stepped out in faith and founded Hearts In Action, Inc. I had absolutely no idea at that time what an amazing journey I was embarking on.

I wrote this book for all of the people who, like me, don't feel they can fill the shoes of someone like Mother Teresa, but have this burning inside to go beyond their everyday lives.

I also wrote this to share with you the wonderful grace and mercy God has shown me by allowing me to be used for His purpose.

As you read these stories, you will find that they are both separate and distinct, and intimately intertwined.

Love Through Me is my heart's prayer. I want to spend my life bringing the love of Christ, in a tangible way, to those to whom others might not go; to touch the untouchable.

I hope you will understand the creative nature of my writing, especially when the "trees" talk to me in "If Only These Trees Could Talk." I asked the Lord to reveal to me a deep sense of what happened there. Many of the stories in this section I pulled from the experiences of people I met and gave them a voice through the trees.

Above all, I hope you will see the heart of a woman who longs to live her life in service to her Lord and Savior. I am an ordinary woman who's witnessed extraordinary grace and love as Christ reaches out, through human hands, to those so precious to Him.

"Religion that God our Father accepts as pure and faultless is this: to look after orphans and widows in their distress and to keep oneself from being polluted by the world."

James 1:27

1

THEY CALL ME SERGEI

Chauffer for a day. That was me. On that sunny June morning, my job was to drive six orphans from Connecticut to Boston to meet their "summer camp" host families. Each of these children would spend the next five weeks with a family who had shown interest in the possibility of adopting them. This journey, which began several months earlier, was one filled with hope. Hope held deep in the hearts of the expectant parents. Hope in the hearts of the orphans visiting from the Ukraine. Hope that someday the children would return to these parents and stay here forever.

The children had spent the previous night in a hotel, awaiting their trip to Boston. As I opened the door to their room, six little bodies crowded the doorway to see who was there. Just me. They all took turns generously doling out hugs and smiles as their chaperone introduced us. I feebly attempted to share my name in their native language. "Natasha," I said, pointing to myself. They laughed and giggled at the funny lady smiling and acting as a human baby-gate in the doorway. I was doing my best to contain the excited tots.

Slowly we ushered them back into the room with hand gestures and gentle voices. Once inside, I met the oldest of the group, a handsome eight-year-old. Polite, yet considerably more cautious with his affection, he greeted me with an outstretched hand. He held my gaze for just a second before averting his eyes to the floor and saying in a firm Ukrainian voice, "They call me Sergei."

I attempted a little interaction but he quickly moved on, taking his backpack and a car seat or two in hand as if to say, "Let's go." Sergei was assuming his rightful role as group leader. I later learned that he was a veteran. Sergei had made this trip last year. He knew the drill and, having been through this before, probably recognized the magnitude of this day.

Over the next few hours, as I drove, Sergei occasionally glanced in the rearview mirror at me with his beautiful blue eyes. I felt drawn to those eyes, as if there were an entire lifetime hidden in there. They were eyes that had seen more than an eight-year-old should. Eyes that now fought to remain dry despite being so far away from the familiarity of the orphanage. Eyes that tried to say, "I'm in charge. I'll be fine." Eyes that unmistakably longed to hope. But the pain of past rejection loomed large in his heart, suppressing the hope, confining it to a barely recognizable glimmer in a sea of blue.

Just after noon we pulled up in front of the adoption agency. Several women standing outside began to smile and giggle and jump up and down and wave as the much-awaited arrival of these precious children was finally here. After brief introductions, each woman took the hand of a child and escorted them up a long flight of stairs to their offices. By the time I parked the van and joined them, they were all settled in the large third-floor conference room.

The room was lined with windows on one side and cabinets on the other. A huge conference table took up much of the space with its dark wood and padded chairs. The large seats enveloped the six tiny children. In addition to their escorts, an interpreter accompanied each child. The host of curious, caring onlookers smiled as big as they could in an attempt to bridge the language gap. Host families were not due to arrive for another hour, but the room full of people, in the meantime, fed, cuddled, and entertained the children.

This was an important hour for the children. It was their opportunity to rest and regroup. Their flight had left the Ukraine more than 24 hours earlier. It had been a full turn of the clock filled with layovers, a hotel stay, and stranger after stranger sent to greet them and lead them to the next destination. Even the most seasoned traveler would have been exhausted by now. These travelers ranged from Sergei, 8 years old, strong and confident (at least on the outside), to Alexandra, only 4, tiny, fragile, and fear dripping off almost every part of her body.

Each child found a brightly colored gift bag, custom prepared and overflowing with stuffed animals and carefully chosen toys, on the table. Their eyes sparkled as they realized that these gifts were for them. They were "for keeps," something they knew little about.

The spread before them also included applesauce and crackers, juice boxes and bagels. The escorts spoon-fed some children while they simply removed the wrappers for others. These toys, food, smiles, and hugs were more than some of the children had ever experienced.

Then there was Sergei. Alone in his chair. Staring straight ahead. It was as if he couldn't even watch the others. They had attention being heaped on them from every direction, while he sat in agonizing isolation. You see, Sergei's host family was able to speak a little bit of Ukrainian. This would be a blessing once they arrived. However, for the next hour the blessing would be a detriment as he was the only one without an interpreter at his side. And without an interpreter, all the well-meaning, English-speaking adults were absent as well.

I pulled my chair alongside his and said hello again. Carefully opening his applesauce and other snacks, I reverted to sign language in an effort to help him understand. I held the applesauce container in my left hand while clumsily motioning with the spoon in my right as if I were going to eat his applesauce. I lifted the spoon several times from the applesauce to my mouth, each time licking my lips and smiling with delight as if it was the best thing I had ever pretended to taste. I let out an intentional but playful laugh. He responded with continued silence. Silly, desperate smiles shot across my face as I longed to be able to speak to him. A gentle pat on the back, a tussle of his hair, all attempts to let him know he was not alone, or unloved. I called to Christina, a volunteer interpreter, and asked if she would sit with him and talk to him. She gladly pulled up a chair.

Christina, using her very best motherly voice, along with his familiar Ukrainian language, spoke to Sergei. Using caring, soft words she tried to comfort him. She told him how happy we were he was with us. She expressed the excitement of meeting his host family. She asked him how he was doing. He sat in silence. Silence not from a discourteous child, but from an inability to do anything more. His eyes bore a hole in the wall ahead of him. Neither to the left nor the right did they wander. The entire weight of his world was resting on him as he sat there in anticipation of the family that would come to take him home. He would try to work hard and be helpful. He would be polite, smile, and not make any messes. He would not bother them at night with the fears that spill out of his eyes in the dark. But would it be enough?

"Aren't you hungry?" Christina asked Sergei. A slight shake of his head indicated that he wasn't. But that wasn't entirely true. He was hungry though not so much for the food that was before him. Sergei's hunger originated from a place much deeper than his stomach. It was firmly rooted deep inside his heart and grew to fill him body and soul until he dared not speak lest he burst. His was a hunger that could only be satisfied by the loving acceptance of a forever family.

The excited families began arriving around 1:00 p.m. Host mothers tried to be calm and refined, yet couldn't resist taking a peek in the door to see if they could catch a first glimpse of their child. The look in their eyes was so familiar to me. Memories flooded my heart. My mind transported me back.

April, 1996, Seoul, South Korea, my husband and I sat anxiously awaiting our first glimpse of our son. The warm people that occupied the desks sat in stark contrast to the cold, utilitarian metal furniture that filled the large, dimly lit room. It was clean, and in good repair, but with just enough comfort to be used for its appointed purpose, the intake and release of Korean orphans. Sounds so foreign to us filled the office in which we sat. Even now as I write I laugh at the irony, for my memories remind me how, back then, *we* were the recipients of those sincere but awkward smiles trying to break the language barrier. This was one of the most exciting days of my life, and I could sense the desire of the other people in the room to be part of our blessing. We were able to share that moment with them but communicated only through our eyes. Previously I had heard the saying that the eyes are "a window to the soul," but I knew little about the depth of those words until that day.

People bustled around us as we sat for what seemed like an eternity. Then I spotted an older woman with dark hair and a kind, rounded face walking right past us to the other side of the room. She appeared to be inquiring as to where she should go. I remember staring at the little boy wrapped in cloth, resting on her back, and wondering, "Is this our son?" What a strange thing to ponder! And what a strange sight. I've seen baby carriers before but most of the ones I've seen cuddle the child on the front of the mom's body. As strange as it seemed, this Korean baby carrier was clearly far more practical. This simple cloth enveloped the child and his foster mom with a loving sense of security, while still allowing her both hands free to carry her groceries, clean her house, or whatever else she needs to do. We may have thought it strange, but the beautiful toddler she was carrying rested peacefully on her back.

Just then someone pointed her in our direction, and as they began the painfully long walk across the room to where we sat, our social worker whispered words I will never forget, "I think this is your son." What a peculiar yet amazing feeling! What an incredibly powerful whisper! I could almost see my husband's heart leap from his chest as he first laid eyes upon his new baby boy.

Eventually, the woman reached us and was offered a seat that had been turned toward us, completing our family circle. She sat with our son on her lap. He smiled at us occasionally, and seemed to be trying to figure out what was happening. We all laughed when he purposefully closed his eyes as if maybe we couldn't see him. He'd check periodically to see if we were still there. Eventually sleep overtook the toddler and naptime prevailed.

I could sense the older woman was processing a myriad of emotions. She was, in my estimation, an amazing woman. She had loved and cared for this little boy since he was 10 days old, and there was no doubt the care had been exceptional. Their bond was evidence of that.

In this world today there are more than 35 million parentless children. War, famine, AIDS, poverty, and even selfishness, all can rob children of their biological families. "Sub-standard" would be a generous word for many of the orphanages available to these children. Even if the children are blessed with loving caregivers, there is often not enough food, clean water, and clothing to meet their most basic needs. Some are blessed to live in a foster home, which ideally offers them a less institutional setting. However, sometimes those children are reminded of their temporary status as a family member. They are kept at arm's length, often unintentionally, to protect the hearts of the foster family. Still others fall victim to even more egregious abuses and injustices.

But our son was truly blessed by God. He spent those first 21 months in a loving family, being cared for by an outstanding foster mother and father. In his culture, the entire family sleeps on the floor together. The father typically sleeps closest to the door, a symbol of his pro-tective nature. The children and mother then find their rightful places on the mat next to him. Our son, as we understand, slept next to his foster father. He was blessed to receive not only food and clothing, but also emotional support and a sense of belonging.

Many times adoptive parents face challenges as their children have to learn how to love and be loved. Attach-ment issues can be painful for all involved. Not only was John loved in that family, but he was taught to love back. This was a wonderful gift to him and would prove to be an invaluable gift to us as well. Surely his children and their children will also reap the fruit she sowed as he shares that love with them, too. For almost two years they extended their hearts and lives to him. Yet all the while, this incredible foster mother prayed for a permanent home for him.

I am reminded of a poem I once heard that says some people come into our lives for a reason. They are only there temporarily, but serve a need for the time they are with us. Some people stay with us for a season. We learn and love and grow with them, but eventually circumstances take them from us. Then there are some who are with us for a lifetime, enjoying a shared journey together. This beautiful woman came into John's life for a reason. Selflessly she stayed for just a season, but her ministry will affect lifetimes.

One by one, children took the hand of their interpreter, who escorted them into the room where, for the first time, they met their host family. Anticipation filled the air as smiles and tears intermingled with each meeting. Jeremiah and Emily went first. Then came Sergei's turn. A kind, older woman took him by the hand and led him down the hall to that fateful meeting place.

The air surrounding Sergei was somehow heavier than anywhere else in the entire building. He could hardly breathe. At only eight years old, he was a major participant in a life-changing meeting. His life! And he knew it. Memories of last year flooded his mind. Memories of returning to the orphanage with other children who shared wonderful stories of the parents who had promised to come for them, memories of his host parents who had not made those promises to him. Still, for quite some time he had hoped. He wondered if he had just missed those promises, maybe because of the language differences. Then came the gut-wrenching realization that the other children were gone. They had all gone "home." But no one had come for him. He was, once again, abandoned. Such memories had haunted him these past months and now they attacked him full force as if it was only yesterday.

His heart pounded. His mind raced. Could he bear to go through that again? Could his little heart take the pressure of trying to figure out what he'd done wrong last time? Couldn't somebody please just tell him so he wouldn't do it again?

Sergei could feel the pressure build inside his body until it finally burst out and tears exploded from everywhere. It was time to go home with this new couple, and though they were patient and kind, Sergei knew he couldn't do it alone.

"Which one of you is closest to Sergei? Which one had the most interaction with him this weekend?" The adoption coordinator burst through the conference room door and fired questions at us in an attempt to throw Sergei a lifeline. For a brief moment we stared at each other like deer in the headlights. "Which one?" she pleaded.

Vera, with only three years in this country herself, stepped forward as the best candidate for the job. After very little discussion, Vera returned to the meeting room and gently took Sergei by the hand. Kneeling down to meet him face-to-face, she promised to go with him to the new house. She promised to stay with him for awhile until he found his way around. Sergei drew a deep, brave breath and dried his eyes. Too fatigued to continue on as a brave soldier, he did his very best to at least not let the tears spill out again. He took one last deep breath, tightened his lips slightly, and gave a quick but firm nod of his blonde head. Still silent, he followed Vera's lead. They left the building hand in hand, his host parents nervously leading the way.

Those of us who were left behind worried, and prayed, and cried, and prayed again.

We allowed 40 minutes or more to pass before leaving to pick up Vera. My mind raced. Would that be enough time? Would

Sergei adjust? Would he be okay when she had to leave? What must this precious, patient couple be thinking? What would we find when we got there?

What we found when we arrived was a young boy who had, to some degree, allowed his defenses to be lowered. The air around him was lighter. He was racing about freely from room to room of this English Tudor home. "Dickens" was following him about. Dickens was Sergei's new puppy, about the size of a loaf of bread, with white curly hair. Mutual curiosity led them to each other. Mutual longing held them there. Neither of them would be alone now. Named after Charles Dickens, this friendly four-legged creature had somehow found the little boy hidden inside the veteran.

Vera sent a knowing smile our way as our expressions asked if everything was okay. The couple greeted Christina and me with smiles that revealed guarded relief, and invited us to finish up the tour of the house with them. We entered a room about 20 by 20 that housed a number of exercise machines; treadmills, stair climbers, stationary bikes. Row after row of books framed the room. Hundreds of them! Classics and contemporaries alike. This room was designed to keep one healthy, body and mind. Both equally important. Both equally represented. All available to their young visitor.

Once again Sergei engaged me with his big, blue, now sparkling eyes. Somehow they told me he wanted me to follow him. He led me up the staircase, pausing briefly at the top to wait for me to catch up. Then he headed straight for a room off the right corner of the hall. He sat proudly on the bed. His bed. This is his room. The smile returned to his face and told me to look around. "This is all for me!" he thought loudly enough for me to hear.

They had filled his closet with clothes. Just his size! They had filled shelf after shelf with age-appropriate books. They had covered his mattress with clean sheets and blankets that smelled fresh and felt soft and new. But it wasn't the thought of having these things that meant the most to him. It was knowing that they had prepared for his coming, that they were ready for him. This realization removed the barriers on his heart, allowing hope to grow at last. "This," he imagined, "must be what 'home' feels like."

We finished our tour and I nervously awaited telling Sergei that we had to leave and, more importantly, that we needed to take Vera with us. He asked her something I couldn't understand, and I secretly feared that he was asking her to stay. But I was wrong. He just wanted her to remind him of the dog's name. "Deekins," he said happily. "Deekins, Deekins," he repeated as he ran in circles, summoning his new buddy to follow him inside. Dickens obliged.

Vera promised both Sergei and his host family she would call to check in on him. The sweet, gentle man pleaded with her not to forget, for Sergei's sake. "It will mean so much to him."

We all waved good-bye. Our leaving was barely noticed by the duo dancing and jumping around each other in the doorway. But that was fine with us. It is a rare occasion in life when we don't want to be missed. And rarer still, a time when we are blessed to witness the transformation of a life.

Sergei, along with four of his travel buddies, found their forever families that week. He did have to go back to the orphanage for a short time while the paperwork was done, but this time he had been given that promise, and there was no mistaking it, soon he'd be coming back home.

As I drove them back to Connecticut, the change in Sergei was so evident. He was a child again. He climbed the rope ladder and slid down the slide on the playscape when we stopped for a break in the ride. He laughed and ran and joked with the freedom of a boy who knew what it was like to be wanted, to be loved.

I've often mused about meeting Sergei and his family again someday. I imagine a little boy where a soldier once stood. I see a loving father and mother who can hardly believe the blessings that fill their home and their lives now that he's there to stay. As Sergei sees me, he and his snow-white, curly-haired dog run to greet me. He tells Dickens to sit and I realize his English is very good, with just a slight hint of his accent–no doubt thanks to the caring teaching of his parents. Sergei and Dickens entertain us with all the tricks Sergei has taught him.

Sergei has grown, but not just physically. He is somehow softer and stronger all at once. He has the obvious signs of someone who is loved deeply, and knows it. He is no longer surviving–he is thriving.

In my mind's eye, as Sergei comes closer, I am awestruck by the changes I see. Hope has finally flourished in him. Those deep blue eyes I remember from our first day together seem even bigger and brighter with the joy that lives inside. This time a smile accompanies a gentle, lingering handshake as he looks me straight in the eyes and says, "They used to call me Sergei. Now they call me son."

"What if there's a bigger picture? What if I'm missing out?
What if there's a greater purpose I could be living right now?
I don't want to miss what matters. I want to be reaching out.
Show me the greater purpose, so I could start livin' right now,
Outside my own little world."

"My Own Little World" – Matthew West

2

HEARTS IN ACTION

It started out just like any other Tuesday. Nothing special. Just the usual morning rush of a working mother: up at six, dress and feed my little guy, drop him off at school, and head into my "sometimes I love my job, sometimes I hate my job" world like so many others.

It had been about six months since I started my position as Program Coordinator. I had originally applied to be their Office Manager on the for-profit side of the business, a land-developing company. At the time of the interview the owner asked if I'd mind helping out with their nonprofit a few hours a week as well. Little did he know that the nonprofit side, which was established to help orphans find families, was the most exciting part of the job for me.

Somewhere in between filing and typing and researching an orphanage in Uganda, the phone's ring interrupted my focus. I reached for the receiver, sure I was going to take a message for the boss and get back to my work. I had no idea that my entire life was about to change.

On the other end of the phone was the voice of a man with an unfamiliar accent. I was certain it was African, but not sure which country. He introduced himself, Dennis, and proceeded to tell me he'd seen our website online. He shared his story with me, one that will never leave me.

Dennis was from Sierra Leone. He told me of his travels on foot from one village to another trying to feed children who had been abandoned or orphaned by the horrendous civil war. He would carry rice or whatever he could get to three different villages, finding children sleeping in the bushes, or right out in the open on the dirt road, and feeding them for that day. He continued this day after day, but with little to no resources himself, and a family of his own to feed, he was looking for someone to partner with him. The purpose of his call was to ask for 100 US dollars to help him buy food. Freetown, Sierra Leone to Connecticut, United States— the phone lines connected two people for a purpose, and created friends for life.

I knew I had to try to help, but it wasn't my decision to make. I also knew my boss' land-developing company had just made a seriously successful deal, netting him a huge seven-figure profit. What excellent timing! How would he even miss $100?

When Roger returned to the office that afternoon I told him of the call and asked if we could wire $100 to help. He said that would be fine as long as I got the correct contact information and confirmed where to send it. I almost flew out of his office without touching the ground! I had instructed Dennis to call back the next day and could hardly wait for the chance to tell him we would help.

The next morning I waited anxiously for the phone to ring. Was this a dream? Was it real? Would he call back? As instructed, he called and I was able to gather the information I needed to give to my boss. I went to lunch with the intention of transferring the money that afternoon.

When I got back from lunch, Roger grumbled, "That guy from Africa called. I can hardly understand him." He seemed almost angry. Whatever. I could understand Dennis just fine. I told Roger that I had gotten the needed information. He stalled by saying I had to wait until the next day when his accountant was in. I took a deep breath and agreed to work with her in the morning. I hated to make Dennis wait, but what was one more day?

Thursday came and went without the funding. Roger's accountant, Cheryl, had come in that day and I told her all about this exciting new partnership, but still they weren't ready to send the money. Friday didn't look any more promising. Finally Roger told me he'd decided not to work with Dennis because that part of the world is too corrupt and he couldn't be sure this wasn't just a scam. Frustration began boiling just under the surface of my skin like an old tin coffee pot on an open flame. I already promised him the money. This was a good cause, and I had given my word. I wanted to explode, but I didn't. Calmly I asked, "If I am able to confirm this is legitimate, can we help them?" Roger assured me we could. Looking back, my guess is that he never expected that to be possible. But all things are possible with God!

I went to work online and on the phone until I connected with World Vision's International Headquarters. World Vision is one of the biggest, most successful charitable organizations in the world. I was able to get contact information for their representative in Freetown. He was a kind man, thankful that someone was trying to help this needy people, his needy people. He agreed to meet with Dennis and look into the work he was doing. Not only did he meet with Dennis, he also met with one of the elders of the village, the local pastor, and saw some of the children they were trying to take care of. He eagerly emailed his report and I love the way he worded it. He said, "They are about a good work here in my country."

With great pleasure I ran in to tell Roger the good news. He barely looked up at me as he grunted his response, "OK."

"So we can do it then?" I asked.

"Just get a check from Cheryl," he replied. Not exactly the enthusiasm I was hoping for, but we had done it! I emailed Dennis that day to tell him it was finally approved and I just needed a day or two to get the money.

Almost a week had passed since I first talked to Dennis. That may not seem like a long time, unless you're waiting for food. Cheryl came in and I asked her to cut the check that morning so I could get this taken care of once and for all. She stared at the floor, avoiding my eyes, and told me Roger had told her not to do it. Needless to say, the pot boiled over at this point and I marched into Roger's office for an explanation. He told me a lot of things that afternoon. Some that I could understand. Not necessarily agree with, but understand. For instance, he explained how a nonprofit was bound by their Mission Statement and his didn't include humanitarian aid. It was designed to promote international adoptions. He told me how his Board would never allow him to work in this manner since it had nothing to do with getting those kids adopted.

"So, let's try to find homes for these children, too," I suggested. Such an easy solution. I couldn't see the problem. He then explained that he was not going to send any money to Sierra Leone. I'm not sure if he thought I'd just give up eventually, but he never did intend to send it. I struggled to understand. Our conversation, and all of his explanations, did not help. I had given my word. Now, he refused to fulfill his promise so I was unable to fulfill mine. I wasn't sure at that time whether I wanted to lash out violently, or crumble to the floor. I did neither. I simply walked out; knowing my time in that job was coming to an end.

I must confess I arrived home that night with such anger in my heart. I cried out to God, literally. I cried with such righteous indignation. "What is wrong with him? Why won't he help? Why can't you make him love these children the way I have come to?" It was at that moment I heard a voice, not audibly, but clear as anything I've ever heard before or since. He simply said, "I didn't put these children on his heart, Natalie. I put them on yours. Now go do something about it."

I knew I had to take what God had laid on my heart and put it into action. I vowed to do so from that moment forward. That was the moment Hearts In Action was born.

A few weeks later in August of 2004, I stepped out into a new career and a new world: insurance sales. I took the exam and became an Independent Insurance Representative. For those of you unfamiliar with the meaning of "Independent," in this case it means straight commission. I was petrified! I had never sold anything before, other than a few wicker baskets or Pampered Chef, but nothing in this realm or even close. I had also never worked on straight commission before. I knew, however, that I needed two things from this new career. First, I needed to make sure I could earn above and beyond what I had been making before. If I worked hard, I earned more. If I slacked off, I earned less. No limits on what I could do. Second, but no less important, I needed flexibility in my schedule. Being an independent insurance representative gave me both, so I jumped in with both feet balancing my new career and my passion for helping children, and I've never looked back.

My first task with Hearts In Action, of course, was to turn to my friends and raise that first $100 for Dennis and the children of Sierra Leone. With great joy I sent him the money and watched as he communicated what the Lord was doing in and through us. My oldest son, Justin, volunteered to handle the administrative work and we were off and running.

I continued my research which now included setting up a 501(c)3 nonprofit organization. I realized how much I had learned working with Roger the past year. I understood rules and regulations that I had never even heard of before because of helping him. Still, there was much more to learn, and I began researching about poverty, children, organizational requirements, as well as the country of Sierra Leone itself.

Prior to Dennis' call I knew very little about Sierra Leone. I needed to learn more about this civil war he spoke of. What I found was the stuff nightmares are made of. Or should I say Hollywood movies? (If you'd like to watch a powerful movie based on true events within Sierra Leone, see "Blood Diamonds." It is very violent, so not suitable for children. If you do watch it, however, please remember my children who lived through what you will see.) Without going into all the gory details, this was a war that lasted ten years. Truthfully, Sierra Leone has a whole history of civil unrest and violence. This was just the latest, and maybe most horrific.

For reasons unknown to me at the time, as I researched Sierra Leone, I kept coming across information about Haiti as well. I began to wonder, "Where is the saddest place in the world?" Story after story of poverty, violence, and natural disasters came to my attention. "Surely," I thought with each reading, "this must be the saddest place in the world." Then I realized I was wrong. The saddest place in the world cannot be found on a map, or pointed to on a globe. The saddest place in the world is in the heart of a child without hope.

For the remainder of 2004 we collected and sent the money to feed the children Dennis was taking care of. The number kept growing, as did the donations. Then, in 2005 we broke ground on the Home of Hope Children's Home in Kamasassa Village in Sierra Leone. It was a joint effort from both sides of the world. Dennis was able to make contact with World Orphans here in the states. He began dialogue with them and I took over the conversation with their executive director and handled things from this end. World Orphans generously donated $5,000 for the building materials. Hearts In Action was responsible for raising the funding for labor costs. The men of the villages came together and gave their best effort to build a four-room cinder block home for the seventeen children we had come to care for.

As we undertook this first major project, the Lord was working on my heart, clarifying His call for me. In the past, *missionary*, to me, meant someone who moved his family far away to live in a hut and learned to speak some strange language while hoping to be accepted by the native people. I had never seen myself as someone who could fulfill that.

I have come to see that while we are all called to take part in His Mission, there are a variety of ways we live that out. I believe with all of my heart that I am one that is called to go. I am called to reach out with human hands and divine love to those whom others may not reach, to love those whom others find unlovable. I am also called to bring others with me, whether in person or in the form of their prayer and financial support. And I am called to share my experiences with others, that they might know His call, too.

Building the Home of Hope Children's Orphanage was a huge project, and there were many people involved in raising funds for it. The youth group of St. Mary of Czestochowa church in Middletown, Connecticut raised much of the needed money by coming together and fasting for 24 hours! Imagine 38 teenagers giving up food for an entire day to help children across the globe in Sierra Leone.

Since St. Mary Church also has a school for children grades Pre-K through eight, I began creating interdisciplinary curriculum that could be used in Christian schools, as well as programs and projects that could be used in churches The curriculum included visits from my moose puppet, Mortermer, who shared stories about his friends at the Home of Hope Children's Orphanage. We also included videos that helped communicate the deep needs of children living in Sierra Leone and other third world countries. As mentioned earlier, there was a challenge to youth groups to put their own hearts into action and sacrifice their comfort while giving them an opportunity to raise money for those who have so much less than them. At St. Mary's alone, between the school and the youth group we raised $4,000. That was not all, though. It wasn't just about raising money. It was about raising missionaries.

I believe we made a difference in the hearts and lives of the children at St. Mary School. They stopped me many times in the hall and asked questions about how "my kids" were doing. Students asked if Mortermer, my puppet, was coming in to visit again and tell them about the children in the orphanage. Students and parents alike told me how they prayed as a family for the children in Sierra Leone. My heart overflows when I realize that with one simple program we can impact lives whether in the US or Sierra Leone. One memory in particular, has stayed with me for all these years.

While visiting the sixth grade class, I noticed a beautiful blonde girl sitting a row or two to my left, taking in every word. I knew she was not just listening, but hearing the message of hope for these children. When I was almost finished, I asked if anyone had questions or wanted to say something. She stood up at her desk, choked back the sobs created by the tears streaming down her face, and said, "I can help. I know I'm young, but I can help. I want to help." She then went on to explain her plan for taking this information into the school where her mother worked and asking others to help as well. Kindred tears fill my eyes as I remember a heart touched, a life changed.

Another church, St. Rose in Newtown, Connecticut, opened their doors and hearts to us as we worked with the children and youth. I so enjoyed watching their eyes as they heard from Mortermer. It was such a gift for me to be able to be used in this way. Once, as I was coming down the escalator in a department store, I heard a young boy's voice yell out, "Look! It's Mortermer's mommy!" The connection was wonderful as together Mortermer and I told stories of the children in the orphanage.

One such story was of the youngest girl, Ndamoh. She was brought to the orphanage at only two months old. Malnutrition had caused several physical problems, including such weakened muscles that her eyes were even crossed. This was just prior to our partnering with them. A year later, in a letter entitled, "Life Change Story," Dennis wrote, "…And there were no relatives to give proper care, so the family decided to hand her to the ministry at the age of two months. But still, there was not enough food at the ministry to provide for Ndamoh and other children in the orphanage, but we thank God for our faithful partner (Hearts In Action) and our sister in Christ, Natalie Ryan, for providing rich food for Ndamoh and others."

What a beautiful story. At the time he wrote that Ndamoh was 14 months old and was feeding herself and running and playing with the rest of the children. God is so good!

It was stories like this that inspired children to work and pray in order to help the children at our orphanage. Among the most faithful are a couple of families that came from our own parish, St. Coleman, in Durham, Connecticut. During the time we lived there, Father Greg and the people of St. Coleman were dedicated and faithful both in prayer and financial support. So many beautiful people donated every month and were the lifeblood of our ministry. One family in particular touched my heart and continues to do so.

The DeVille family reached out immediately to support our work. The family began donating monthly and has continued to do so faithfully. But it didn't stop there! Their sons, Geoffrey and Ryan, started a tradition that their daughter, Meaghan, continues to this day. The first year we partnered with St. Coleman, the boys asked their friends to bring donations for Hearts In Action to their birthday party instead of gifts. I was amazed by such a generous idea! Meaghan followed suit and now, every year when it is her birthday,

Meaghan requests the same of her friends who come to celebrate. Every year! We don't ask. We don't remind her. She always comes through. Her faithfulness and her friends' generosity have raised a few thousand dollars to help feed and care for our children. What a blessing Meaghan and her family have been to the children, and to me! At Hearts In Action, our dream is that no child should go to bed with the pain of hunger in their belly, or with the fear of violence in their hearts. The DeVille family is helping us realize that dream wherever we go.

"But you will receive power when the Holy Spirit comes upon you. You will be witnesses to me in Jerusalem, in all Judea, in Samaria, and to the uttermost parts of the earth." Acts 1

I had been given so many opportunities to teach and speak and work with people of all generations. I spoke at board meetings, women's meetings, schools, churches, to youth groups, to elementary school children, and even to a quilters' group at a Congregational Church. Up until that point, however, they had been separate groups of separate ages at separate times. I began thinking about how to have an intergenerational project. What came of that ended up being not only intergenerational, but interdenominational as well.

The children of St. Rose parish ranged in ages from Pre-K through eighth grade. This presented me with quite a challenge as I prayed about how to utilize each of them in an age appropriate way. I had a myriad of ideas for hands-on help the older children could do, but needed something tangible for the younger grades. Then it hit me. One of my dear friends went out and bought a variety of fabrics with vibrant colors, like the ones she imagined you'd see in Africa. In fact, one pattern included a village scene with a small hut and a woman carrying a basket on her head. We cut the material into squares and gave the children lots of different things they could use to decorate their square. Some simply colored on them with markers. Some used other pieces of fabric, felt, or yarn to dress theirs up. Some made tiny giraffes and huts. Others made crosses. Many wrote messages on their square like "we love you" or "Jesus loves you."

Once the squares were completed, Mortermer and I collected them and brought them across the state to the women of Hebron Congregational Church. Their incredibly talented quilters' group went to work sewing the squares together and made 18 quilts! They were beautiful. Some of those quilts were used to thank people or groups who had made significant contributions to our mission. Others were sold to raise money for food for the children at the orphanage. One still hangs on my wall to this day. It was a wonderful experience and I pray we will be able to do something similar again someday.

As exciting as it was working with all these different people to help meet the needs of the children of Home of Hope Orphanage, I was also aware that there are needs much closer to home. I remembered the scripture in Acts 1 that talks about being His witnesses "in Jerusalem, all Judea, Samaria, and to the uttermost parts of the earth." I had always been taught that meant we are to reach out locally, regionally, nationally, and internationally. Obviously the latter was covered, but I didn't want to neglect the rest. I began keeping my eyes and heart open for opportunities to be involved on a local level. Since my time was quite full between my job and Hearts In Action, I knew I couldn't take on any long-term responsibilities, but stayed open to being a gap filler. If there was a need for one more server at the soup kitchen one week, I'd fill that gap. If there was a need for more toys for the Christmas collection, or coats for the coat drive, I'd fill that gap. I even organized a business clothing drive with my friends at work and one generous man donated thousands of dollars' worth of dress shirts for people trying to get

back in to the workforce. Not quite the front line work I was longing for, but I prayed with each outreach that the Lord would bless
someone through our efforts, and His name would be glorified.

Then, in 2005, a terrible hurricane pummeled the gulf coast,
a hurricane named Katrina. The country watched in horror as the
flood waters rose and levies broke, leaving many stranded, while
other perished. A friend of mine from church who had lived in that
area when he was younger gave us updates as he traveled back and
forth with teams from his home church. Bob's heart was broken by
the continued needs of the people there. Selflessly he made five different trips there over a two-year period. He rebuilt homes and
prayed with the people living in them. But the extent of the devastation was so great, there was still much to be done.

Two years later, the effects of the storm were still wreaking
havoc. Whole families were still living in temporary trailers. Houses, or what was left of houses, still sat in crumbled piles in neighborhoods all through the Gulf Coast area. Bob began pulling together another team to head south. Our pastor had asked for prayer
for Bob, and told us how badly he needed helpers to go with him. I
felt a familiar sensation growing inside, just like the one I had when
I first spoke to Dennis years ago. I knew I had to go, but felt confused. What did I have to offer a team of builders? I could swing a
hammer, sure. Thanks to my father, I was even fairly good at putting things together, but that's about it. No one in their right mind
would ever call on me to rebuild part of their house or do heavy
lifting! Bob assured me there was a place for everybody on the team
and that the Lord would provide those who were needed. I spoke
to my husband. Six weeks later I was on a flight to Mississippi,
headed for the front line.

I'll follow you into the homes of the broken.
Follow you into the world.
And meet the needs for the poor and the needy, God.
I'll follow you into the world.

"Follow You" – Brandon Heath

3

IF ONLY THESE TREES COULD TALK

Katrina: Two Years Later

I had just arrived in Mississippi for my first missions trip. It was 26 months after Hurricane Katrina pummeled this area head-on with the fury only a Category 5 storm can bring. I was part of a team gathered to help rebuild some homes in the area.

The ride from the airport to Camp Katrina where we were based was filled with amazing and yet somewhat expected sights: empty lots, piles of rubble where houses once stood, "For Sale" signs, one after another after another. But it was not a messy lot or twisted metal or even a pile of thousand-pound chunks of concrete that captured my attention. It wasn't the  expansive mansions here and there that had already experienced restoration. Instead, I was mesmerized by one small, perfectly green plot of land.

Neat and meticulously groomed, this was obviously a well-cared for yard despite the absence of the house that once stood on it. Even the grass between the tire tracks was mowed on the long straight drive.

To the far left was a small tree on which hung a hunter green porch swing. To the back center of the lot was a beautiful brick staircase with ivy growing up the sides of each step. A bird-bath rested several yards from the bottom stair.

A great, mighty live oak stood to the right of the yard. On the bottom branch, a swing hung with a wooden seat painted in multicolored swirls and two ropes securing it in place. Something grabbed me and told me I must return to this site as soon as I could. I had an overwhelming need to find out more. I continued on to Camp Katrina, knowing I'd be back.

The mighty live oak with the two ropes and wooden multi-colored seat, the brick staircase, and the driveway that leads to no-where–these images haunted me as I tried to sleep that night. I set out the next morning to return to this scene that somehow called out to me. I searched that road until I found it again.

I stepped out of my car, drawn to be part of the picture and understand it better. I walked up those brick stairs and sat staring at that swing. Then I strolled over and rubbed my fingers on the empty seat. I stared up at the tree that held it. One question kept running through my mind: who used to sit on this swing? I gazed up at the mighty oak and thought, apparently out loud, "If only these trees could talk." And so they did.

"She was so precious and bubbly!" the mighty live oak ex-claimed. "Every afternoon she bounded down those front stairs and ran fast as she could to the swing. I braced my branch and held it steady as she scooted on the seat and the two ropes moved ever so gently, first forward then back again. Holding the ropes tight, like the hands of a trusted friend, she stretched her feet as far out in front of her as her legs could take them. Then she leaned back toward the ground behind her, letting her golden curls tickle the grass. And then came the moment I waited for every day. She closed her eyes, like you do just before a sweet kiss, and smiled up at me. I moved my branches back to let the sun caress her face.

"She could swing for hours, that Little Girl. And all the while she serenaded me with songs she'd learned in Sunday school. I could always tell when she'd learned a new one, too. After church, she jumped out of the car as soon as it came to a stop at the end of the drive. She ran over to me and hopped on the swing. The white cotton ruffles on her Sunday dress swayed to and fro as she pumped her little patent leathers to the beat of the song. I'll tell you a secret: sometimes I think she made up some of the words at first. But after a couple more weeks of practice, the words and the tune became more consistent.

"Truth be told, I loved Sundays. Not only did she have endless time to spend with me, but I often noticed her Mom and Dad on the front porch. It was the one day of the week they were sure to sit and rock in their hunter green porch swing and enjoy the blessings before them. Not everyone gets to live on such a beautiful shore. They watched as the warm, summer sun danced off the waves across the street.

"At times I saw them just stand there, Mom with her toes barely touching the top layer of brick that leads from the yard to the porch. Dad embraced her from behind and they swayed together to the rhythm of the sweet, soft music from the speakers they had placed in the window. She leaned her head on the great white pillar to her left as together they marveled at their most precious blessing, Little Girl; swinging and singing and smiling up at me.

"Often they took their big, vanilla ice cream-colored blanket with the cotton candy blue stripe and lay it on the ground between my trunk and the birdbath. Little Girl and Dad talked about their week and shared stories that I am sure were make believe and happened only in their imaginations. I wonder if she thought them up while the swing and I held her, head back and eyes closed and blonde curls tickling the grass. In some ways I hope so. I hope that I was that safe place she could go to dream Little Girl dreams.

"After they ate the scrumptious fried chicken and juicy watermelon Mom prepared, they all stretched out on that blanket and dreamed together. Little Girl laid her head on Dad's chest and Mom held both their hands. They talked about silly things. They talked about sad things. They talked about happy things, and even forever things. And then it happened, Mom looked right at my branches and said, 'I am so grateful we have this big old oak to be near while we share together time. Every family should be so blessed to have such a very special friend.'

"Yes, I love Sundays, or at least I used to, before that terrible day. Now, no one swings here anymore. The driveway is empty, and the porch is no longer here. The porch, the house, and the speakers in the windows with the sweet, soft music are all gone. I don't know where. Even my top, way up high branches can't see them. The only things that are left are the hunter green porch swing which Dad put in that tree over there, the brick staircase that leads from the yard to nothing, the bird bath with silt residue and no birds, and the swing. The quiet, lonely swing. Sometimes I move my branch ever so slightly and we, the swing and I, pretend she's come back to us. Our imaginations bring her back to swing and sing and smile up at us. But that's just in our imaginations. It's our own make believe."

I turned my eyes toward his friends, wondering if they understood. One of the pines said, "I remember that day." Suddenly every tree I saw wanted to tell me his story. It was as if they were all vying for my attention, like young children wanting to tell me their version of the story, or old men needing to.

"We still don't know what made the wind and the sea so angry," said the pine. "This wasn't the first time they ganged up on us, but we had never seen them *this* angry. Never had we seen such a fierce and violent demonstration of their power. The rains came, too. But we've had rain before. Then, without warning the wind swirled around behind the sea and pushed it so that it lunged at us. The sea covered the land, and many of us. Some of us have been growing here for hundreds of years, and still the water covered our tops. Some of us stood up on our tiptoes to try to reach above the flood, but tiptoes are not so steady, and we fell under the pressure. Still others were surrounded by the wind, and as it swirled its circular fury, we became dizzy and weakened and bent in submission."

"Like him," a scruffy pine said pointing to the old live oak, "many of us had families before that day. Our families lived beneath our branches. They played on our swings or rested in our shadows. Some built forts in our branches. Others carved their initials surrounded by hearts in our trunks—a sign of their forever-ness, forever a part of us.

"Some of our families left before the fury. We wondered how it was that so many could be taking a vacation at once, but no one told us why.

"Still other families stayed. It is for those we still weep. As the water rose, they climbed higher and higher in their houses, trying to get away. But like an evil villain it kept chasing them. Some people kicked holes in their roofs and climbed out to safety. Some roofs were still not tall enough."

A tender, young oak told me how the couple that lived beneath his branches ran in just this way to safety on their roof. "I saw his foot come through the roof and then he lifted his wife out to safety. I could still see the water rising through the windows as he dove in the water to get the two dogs that rested in my shade every morning. The little black one came first and with the man's help he joined his lady on the roof. Then, to my surprise, I spotted the big yellow lab under the water in the first floor. He didn't know how to get to the top of the house and the swirling current kept confusing him. His master took a deep breath and pushed himself back under the water, pulling himself farther and farther below the water to reach him. Then his master hugged him from the middle and pulled him to the roof. Despite the continual pounding of wind and waves, I celebrated for just a minute as he and his wife joined in a triumphant embrace.

"The celebration, however, was short-lived. Within seconds their embrace turned from triumph to tragedy. I could see it in the way they clutched each other. I could see it in the way they suddenly fell into a heap and cried out almost uncontrollably in disbelief. I could see it in their eyes, and I followed their gaze to the source of their agony. Horrified they watched, we watched, as their neighbors passed by. Not in their bright blue Buick as usual, with a honk and a wave. But one by one they floated by. Lifeless and just out of reach.

"Just then I noticed another man, a neighbor from the next block. He was in the water, too, but not lifeless. He was fighting, reaching, for someone, something. In the middle of the wind, I stretched out my branches and caught him. He held tight to me until the waters receded. Exhausted and too high up to get down on his own, he stayed there for eight days until the man and his wife and the black and yellow labs stepped out onto their porch. I don't know what made them look up, but they did. This time there was life. This time there was hope. This time they were able to help. And this time the victorious embrace lasted for a very long time."

I wandered, stunned and saddened by what the trees had told me. I found myself in a small grove with a smattering of trees. A couple of mighty live oaks dominated. There were a few pines as well, and one magnolia bush, misshapen and desperate for attention. Below the trees was mostly barren ground. Patches of grass sprung up here and there, but without anyone to care for and nurture them, most gave way to hardened, lifeless dirt and crunchy, dried out leaves the trees were no longer able to hold on to.

The grove was ominously close to the water's edge and even then I could feel the sea breeze trying to intimidate me. With the exception of a few bent pylons and a pile or two of crumbled pavement, you'd never know anyone had ever lived there. Sure there were two staircases on the block, but they led to nowhere. An eerie silence surrounded me. No sign of life could be found. I began to wonder if these trees ever had families, until I looked up. Once they realized I was there, they all began talking at once. "Look at me, look at me," they seemed to be crying, and so, a sort of show-and-tell began.

The first tree showed me a white door. High up in his

branches the door to his family's house perched precariously. He recalled how many times he'd seen his family come in and out of that door. He marveled at how no matter who knocked on that door, and no matter what time of day or night, "Ma'am" answered with a welcoming smile. He relished the days when friends came to visit and there was a steady stream of creaking hinges and slapping doors. For him it was a sign of a good life to have so many uses for a single door.

The next tree showed me a buoy and a bleach bottle that had followed the rigging of its sailboat, along with part of its dock, and came to rest on one of his lower branches. It had been tossed by the nasty wind almost half a mile.

Another had a blue and white print curtain hanging side-ways–not much use now but the tree remembered watching the Mrs. in the house that used to live below him as she made those curtains on her old pedal sewing machine. He could see her smile as she hung them in their new addition to the kitchen. She even splurged and purchased some new dishes to match!

"My family left early. I guess they forgot about me," this tiny little magnolia, bent and sad, didn't even raise herself up as she talked. Even her flowers pointed downward instead of reaching for the sky. "The only thing left of them is this shredded lei left over from their trip to Hawaii. It's been two years, and they haven't even come by to see how I am. I guess I can't blame them. The only people who come here anymore either have cameras in their hands or tears in their eyes–sometimes both."

The sea breeze picked up a bit, and I felt the chill from it and from the stories as well. I began to rush through the grove, turning my back toward the threatening water and heading back toward my parked car, until I was distracted by something flapping in the wind to my right. I walked closer and closer to a tree on the right perimeter of the grove. Dangling from its lower left branch was a long, white sheet.

As the wind whipped about, it snapped over and over. The tree was silent, hoping the white flag would do its bidding for him. After two long years he was tired. He was tired of trying to stand up to the wind. He was tired of the fight to survive. He was tired of waiting for his family to return. He was just plain tired. He wanted to give up, and he hoped the white flag would speak the words of surrender for him.

After a deep, long breath I turned toward my car, full of memories of families I'd never even met: the white door, the buoy, blue and white print curtains. And there were so many others: the paisley bedspread, the quilted mattress top, a piece of canvas ripped from the mast of a boat in the cove. One after one they kept talking. They wouldn't let me get back to my car.

Suddenly, and without warning, a tree from the side of the road stopped me in my tracks. It was another large, live oak. I stood in awe at his show-and-tell display. I wanted to cry, but I couldn't. I could only stand there and listen. At the base of the tree was a pillow. A standard size, like you'd find on a twin bed. It was naked of any pillowcase and lay in the dirt. I stared at it for the  longest time, until he begged me to look higher.

A teal green shredded window curtain danced in the wind. To the left of it, two other items. One was a bed sheet, white with crimson flowers. Before I could study the other item, the tree spoke to me again.

 "I had never had a family of my own," the tree told me. "I live too close to the road. That's why I was so shocked when, in the midst of the storm, the Mom turned to me and hugged me so tightly. Her face was wet and though I know some of the drops were from the rain, some of them

were salty and hot and full of pain. She had wrapped her daughter in a blanket. Mom and Little Girl clung to me as long as they could. Little Girl's blonde curls were soaked and slapped against her skin in the angry wind. I tried to turn in such a way as to protect them but suddenly they were gone. I never did see where they went. I've held onto this blanket for all this time, hoping they'll come back for it. "

I began to convulse as tears overpowered me. The mighty live oak and the lonely wooden swing flashed through my mind as I gazed up at the blanket. The vanilla ice-cream-colored blanket with a cotton candy blue stripe.

Before leaving for home, I returned one more time to that mighty, live oak, unsure of whether or not to tell him what I knew. He told me that Dad had been there that morning.

"He cleaned off the hunter green porch swing in the tree across the yard. Then he walked pensively to the swing on my branch." The oak whispered in a reverent tone, "He gently held the two ropes in his hands, pulled them back, and gave the seat a little push. Dad turned his face to the ground and wiped away the sadness that had spilled from his eyes. With slow, labored steps he made his way to the stairs, rubbing his fingers along the edge of the birdbath as he passed. At the top of the stairs he sat. For hours and hours he sat. He caressed the top of the bricks where his wife's toes used to touch. And he stared out at the sunshine dancing on the water as if looking for someone."

For a moment, the mighty live oak paused to inhale deeply as if trying to steady his next words. Then he turned away, looking longingly in the direction of the water. When he finally broke the silence his pain was undeniable as he thought, apparently out loud, "I wonder if she'll ever return. I sure do miss her, my Little Girl. She's the one who used to sit on this swing."

Epilogue

More than two years after Hurricane Katrina struck this coastal community, the devastation is still evident. It is evident in the piles of rubble that occupy lot after lot, leaving whole neighborhoods that resemble war zones. It is also evident in the voices of those who used to call that rubble home. Voices that share stories as vivid as if Katrina hit yesterday, and yet with an ache that only years of pain could produce.

I arrived at the Gulfport-Biloxi airport with 10 other people, most of whom I had just met that morning. The ride from the airport to Waveland, Mississippi was breathtaking. Not breathtaking as in how beautiful and amazing a beachfront community can be. Breathtaking as in something had sucked the breath right out of me. Such shock and disbelief had overtaken me that at times I had to force a big, heavy sigh just to make sure to feed my lungs lest they starve, and I collapse in a pile of my own.

We arrived at Camp Katrina late in the afternoon and settled into our bunks before having a quick dinner and turning in for the night. The next morning we met the rest of our team. Another 14 people had arrived at 3:00 a.m. from Wisconsin. Altogether, two dozen people had gathered for a common purpose. People I barely knew, but who shared a love for Christ and a heart for the people of Waveland. People I soon called friends.

We have never known loss like this, nothing of this magnitude, and despite the thousands of relief workers and the hundreds of thousands of hours of demolition, clean up, and rebuilding, there is still so much to do. Maybe that's why the stories just keep coming–because the evidence still stares at them day after day, a cruel reminder of the recent past when their world was washed away by a storm named Katrina.

But there is hope. Hope for healing, hope for restoration. For as long as people of God continue to live out the Great Commission[1], and for as long as we remember we are His hands and feet, there is hope.

Camp Katrina is one of the vehicles God is using to bring hope and healing to this battered community. There faithfully since the second week after the hurricane, this mission has reached hundreds of people by providing everything from food to building supplies to teams of dedicated workers to help rebuild their homes and lives.

From the trees in this story, to the people of the camp, to the "Restoration" we witnessed during our week as Camp Katrina volunteers, the Lord blessed me with a unique understanding of the need, as well as His provision.

---

[1] The *Great Commission* is the instruction of the resurrected Jesus Christ to his disciples to spread his teachings throughout the world.

Therefore, if anyone is in Christ, he is a new creation; the old has gone, the new has come!

2 Corinthians 5:17 NIV

4

RESTORATION

Flight 632, Seat 23D, Atlanta to Gulfport. That's where my journey began. I was part of a missions team headed to Mississippi to help restore homes destroyed by Hurricane Katrina. More than two years after the storm, I wondered if there would be anything substantial left for me to do. I also wanted to write about my experience and wondered if an-yone would still be interested in talking about theirs. Then I met a nurse named Lindsay. She and her friend and colleague, Meagan, were seated in the window and center seats next to me on the plane. They were on their way home from a conference in DC. As is typically found in the south, Lindsay was very friendly and engaging, and I knew immediately I was going to enjoy this leg of my trip.

I soon learned that they were from a small town called Pascagoula, where they were nurses at a local hospital. I didn't want to be rude, or to drudge up the painful past, but I really hoped they would be willing to talk to me about their experiences during and since Hurricane Katrina. It didn't take long for me to find the answer.

Meagan sat in the window seat, and though polite, she soon positioned herself in such a way as to pay more attention to the window than to me. At the urging of her friend, she occasionally nodded or offered one- or two-word answers to my questions, but everything about her said she would just as soon leave Katrina in the past.

As much as Meagan wanted to be left alone, Lindsay was eager to talk and keep me company through the flight. She and I spent the next hour and a half talking like old friends sipping sweet tea on the front porch. I couldn't help but wonder if the Lord was blessing me with an opportunity to learn more about Katrina and to understand the people He would have me minister to. Or was He blessing her with a compassionate ear of someone who truly wanted to hear and know what she had gone through? I now know that both were true.

"It wasn't even supposed to hit us," Lindsay began, "Gulfport, maybe, but not us. Not that far east. But Katrina was like a rebellious child, never doing what was expected of her. She hit, and she hit us hard. The winds were bad enough, but it was the storm surge that got us. I'm not sure what the actual number was. I've heard everything from 14 to 22 feet. All I know is my house wasn't built for that much water. It was completely destroyed, as were the other houses in my neighborhood. We lost everything. And this was the second time for me! In 1999 our house in St. Louis burned to the ground. Not one thing was left. All of our clothes, all of our pictures, every last thing was gone! I guess in a way I am blessed."

"Blessed?" I thought. My thoughts spilled out onto my face and rested in my wrinkled brow. In response to my obvious confusion she explained, "I learned the first time that I could survive such a loss. Things are just things. As horrendous as this was, I knew that as long as I still had my family, I could get through this. Our homes were destroyed, but we were not defeated. Still, I was tired. Bone tired.

"Every day I'd get up and get to work for 5 a.m. The hospital was full. People came in with all kinds of injuries: food poisoning, lacerations, the flu, infections. Most of us, including the hospital, didn't even have a safe water supply. In fact, one of the maintenance staff finally jerry-rigged a pipe system to help us use the duck pond out front for flushing the toilets. I know that sounds crazy, but we needed that small victory. People were so beaten down it was hard for their bodies to heal. For some, just remembering to breathe took all the energy they could muster.

"I don't think I'll ever forget one of my patients. She was recovering from a radical mastectomy when Katrina hit. Her husband kissed her good-bye before leaving to take care of their lovely Victorian home on Beach Boulevard. Their house was on the list of historic homes the town was helping to restore to its former glory, and he wanted to make sure it was protected from the storm.

"Within hours Katrina turned Beach Boulevard into a sort of temporary Atlantis. When the waters finally receded, their two-story Victorian home on a corner lot was nothing more than a pile of concrete and brick-red rubble in the middle of the street. One of the headlines in our local paper quoted a woman as saying, "Beach Boulevard is no more." My patient sat staring at those words for days. She barely moved. She just kept staring at them hoping that somehow the sheer strength of her will could make them change. But of course, they didn't. Nothing she could do would change her desperately lonely new future. Her husband never returned to the hospital. Cancer had taken her breast. Katrina had taken her husband."

We each took a breath as the airline attendant served small packages of cheese-n-crackers and peanuts. Meagan looked up for the first time in over half an hour and ordered a Diet Coke. I just had ice water, not even sure I wanted that much of a distraction. Lindsay offered up a beautiful smile and thanked the attendant for her tomato juice. She took a small sip and a big breath before continuing.

"Every night after work the entire neighborhood gathered at the end of the street in the cul-de-sac. Each of us brought something. One person might have a few vegetables. Someone else might have some bread. Once in a while someone would manage a bit of meat. But no matter what we had, we all brought it to the barbeque. With no stoves or refrigerators, or kitchens for that matter, we all pulled together. Whatever we had, we shared it all."

I marveled at the support these neighbors offered each other in what sounded like a modern day "Stone Soup" story. It was not only a story of sharing, but one of restoration. For as they ate and shared together, their strength was restored for the tasks the evening held for them.

"After dinner we'd all head back to our homes and start rebuilding. You'd be surprised how heavy sheetrock is after working a twelve-hour shift in an understaffed, undersupplied, formerly underwater hospital!"

For once in my life, I hardly spoke a word. Amazed at how strong this gentle woman was, I interjected only a few times with questions. Slowly, and carefully, she cracked open the door of her heart and let me peek inside.

"I'd work until midnight or so and then collapse in my trailer until time to get up and go back to work for 5 a.m. It's not like you could take a vacation day or even a sick day. Those of us who were left had to be there to care for the sick and injured. They needed us, even more than we needed rest."

She told me story after story. Some would break your heart. Some would encourage your spirit. Water and electricity were restored to houses as well as the hospital. Her home was eventually whole again, as were the homes of all her neighbors. Volunteers came in from California to help support the staff and give them much-needed shifts off. With schools and day care centers destroyed, the volunteers even cared for the children of the staff while they worked. After about a year and a half, new nurses and doctors were hired and the hospital began returning to normalcy. Of course, things would never be exactly the same. One would not expect that, after such a catastrophic event. Still, I sensed that despite all the progress that had been made, something still lingered in a damaged state for Nurse Lindsay.

As the Holy Spirit led, I asked if she could tell me her biggest challenge through all this. Suddenly her heart's door swung open wide as she confessed, "I guess the hardest part for me was helping my patients cope with their losses, especially when I'd been up extra late the night before trying to fix the plumbing or rebuild an inside corner of a wall or something. I'd be in a patient's room cleaning out a wound or giving them their medication, and they would cling to me and cry. As a nurse, I understood that there were times when the best thing I could do was hold them and let them cry. Before Katrina, I could sit there and listen and comfort them through the most difficult times. But these days were different. They poured their hearts out and told me about everything they'd lost. They told me how they had nothing left. They looked to me as if there was something I could, or should, do or say to make it better. Sometimes I wanted to scream out, "I lost everything, too. Do you see me? I know you're hurting, but did you ever consider that I am hurting too?" She paused for a moment. "But I couldn't. I wiped the tears from their cheeks, all the while locking my own deep inside." In that moment, I realized that even her close friends, like

Meagan, to whom she might usually go for support, had their own tears to cry.

The sadness of Lindsay's words spilled from both our eyes. Two strangers, who would probably never meet again, joined hearts 30,000 feet in the air. Like a flooded house that must be drained and dried out before it can be restored, so too must be the heart of one so full of unshed tears. As the attendants prepared the cabin for landing, the Lord prepared her heart for a restoration of its own.

♡

As we drove from the airport to Camp Katrina that evening, any concerns I previously held about whether or not we would still be needed were washed away. The devastation from Hurricane Katrina was still evident. There was physical evidence, like piles of concrete rubble, homes crumbled and estranged from their foundations, lots with nothing more than a foundation or some small token to show evidence of families that had once lived there. But it wasn't just the physical evidence that struck me. You could actually still feel Katrina. Her presence was undeniable. In the same way you might feel changes in the barometric pressure during a storm, there was a palpable pressure in the air.

I watched as Bob, our driver, excitedly looked for the progress that had been made since his last trip to Waveland, where the Camp is located. He told us of the bridge we would cross that had been out for over two years. He showed us street after street and home after home that had been devastated. He showed us other areas that had already begun restoration. There was so much to see, too much for one evening. As we continued on toward Camp, he promised another tour in the morning.

On Sunday, we again set out to see the area where we would be working. There was also a small piece of land I had seen the day before that I wanted to revisit. At some point in the afternoon, Bob took a turn down a small side street that led to the water's edge. We were on a small point that was surrounded by water on three sides. In the middle stood a grove of trees, an acre or two still devoid of any reconstruction. From ground level you would never know that anyone had ever lived there. It was nothing but a field of grass and some trees. But if you looked up, you could see debris in each and every tree in the grove. It was an eerie and yet somehow fascinating sight. Like an archeological dig, we found remnants left behind of the people who once inhabited the land.

The road ended at the old ferry landing, not far from that grove. As we turned the car around at the landing, I noticed something bright and colorful near the bushes lining the road. Butterflies! Hundreds of them! They flew in beautiful contrast to the de-struction we'd just witnessed. They filled the bushes and the air and even came to rest on us if we were still long enough. It dawned on me that the things man had built—houses, buildings, boats—were all destroyed. But the things God had created—the trees, the grass, the bushes, and the butterflies—these things thrived. It was not by accident that the Lord showed us these brightly colored beauties. They were a promise from God of His restoration, a foreshadowing of our time at Camp Katrina.

We awoke Monday morning to the sound of a deluge of rain pouring down all around us. But the driving rain couldn't beat down the conquerors we had inside us, knowing the Lord had called us together for a common purpose. While at breakfast each of us received our assignment for the day. Mine was to join several others at the home of the Mayor. Like so many others, his house was destroyed and sat empty on its half-acre piece of land. This dear family had requested that volunteers wait to work on their home until others had received help. Now, more than two years later, they still lived in a FEMA trailer. Mom, Dad, and seven children! From all I had heard about this caring couple, I admired them and was honored to work on their home. I had hoped to meet them at some point and find out more about their Katrina experience, as well as their family.

Full of energy, I jumped from the van I had driven to the site and bounded through the front door of their gutted home. Immediately I came face-to-face with two piles of sheetrock that were chest high on my 5'1" frame. Next to those I encountered a vicious-looking pile of fiberglass insulation. Within seconds I felt my knees knocking and heard the brave warrior inside me screaming, "Run!" There was not a wall in the place. No ceiling either, except for in one room upstairs–and they told us that that one needed to be ripped out and replaced. I kept wondering where the Candid Camera crew was hiding. It must have been comical to watch this slightly-overweight corporate insurance trainer trying to figure out which tool to pick up first. The woman who was used to taking charge didn't even know which floor to start on, let alone how to lead her team through this new adventure.

But that's the great thing about a team. Not everyone needs to lead. In fact, not everyone should. So I looked to the guys with tool belts around their waists and dirt under their fingernails and said, "Teach me." Those who actually knew what to do patiently and lovingly mentored me, and the other novices in the group, all morning. By lunchtime I had plaster in my hair, dirt on my face, and a screw gun in my hand. I was hanging sheetrock! Okay, so I admit I couldn't have done it without a strong, skilled person as my partner–but I had come a long way from that scared, shaking little woman who stood in the doorway a few short hours earlier.

Throughout the day the rain poured as if to remind us of the storm that had called us there. But nothing could stop us. One of our team members was even hanging vinyl siding in the downpour. By quitting time that first evening, Val had learned to "mud," and Vicki and her son had become masters at cutting and piecing sheet-rock into odd-shaped corners and small, dimly lit closets. And I had fallen in love with power tools! We left for our base camp satisfied with and encouraged by our progress.

Once back at camp, and after showering and putting on warm, dry clothes, we shared stories, laughter, and a meal that had been prepared for us by other volunteers.

Ministry unites people like nothing else can. After just one day together, I sensed bonds growing and strengthening within our team. Friendships blossomed and crossed generational and denominational lines. I knew that very day I was among people, former strangers, who would be my lifelong friends. Throughout the week each of us would be challenged in some way. For some of us that began on our first day out. Together we faced those challenges. For the sake of the team, we persevered. With the help of the team, we were victorious.

Still, as we ate dinner together, something was missing for me. As incredible as Monday had been, there was no personal connection for me. Sure, I knew about the family that would inhabit that home, but we'd not yet met. I longed to actually talk to some of the people who'd experienced Katrina to understand the impact on their individual lives, as well as the community. Then I met the potato salad man.

All evening long people had been asking me, "Did you taste the potato salad?" The question was asked so frequently I began to wonder what the big deal was. And for some reason they felt the need to let me know, "Bobby made it." I wondered if these people had ever seen potato salad before. "What's the big deal?" I thought.

You see, I had been focused on the creation, not the creator. It wasn't the potato salad they wanted me to know–it was Bobby.

"Did you get some potato salad?" an older gentleman asked. Before I could answer he added, "I made it." Somehow, despite his quiet and somewhat subdued demeanor, his pride in his potato salad was obvious. He gave us the whole recipe, complete with pickles (like my Mom used to make). Once the recipe was complete, he became introspective for a moment or two. I'm not sure if we asked or if he just overflowed but he began to share his amazing story with us.

Before Katrina, Bobby lived in a beautiful, spacious home. Though he lived there alone, he was proud of that home and enjoyed it very much. His garage was built on a slab, but the house itself was built on stilts, as many shoreline homes are, to protect it from flooding.

At the end of a long day, Bobby could be found in his living room lying on his new couch. He recalled how he had bought that couch not long before the storm. It was his haven, his place of rest. "In fact," he told us, "that sofa was so comfortable that many nights I'd just let myself fall asleep right there."

When warnings of Katrina came, Bobby thought long and hard about whether or not to evacuate. He wasn't stubborn or careless, it's just that he'd planned for this when he built the house. The stilts were there to protect against just such an event. Ultimately, he decided to stay. Bobby's eyes turned downward and for several seconds he sat in silence. We sat patiently until he began again.

"I've never been so scared or shocked in my life," he continued. "As the wind picked up and the floodwaters rose I felt protected in my house on the stilts. Then suddenly, without warning, the wind picked me up–not just me, but my entire house, and threw us 150 feet! When the house landed in the already rising and swirling water, we were swept away. My yard had some trees that bordered the back of it. The house did not stop until it reached those trees. I think the wind was about to flip the house over, but the trees caught us."

When the storm was over and the waters receded, Bobby realized he'd lost almost everything. His house, his car, his garage; so much was gone. He'd escaped with his life, thank God. But the only personal possessions left were the slab from under his garage, and his couch.

Bobby dragged the couch to the slab where his garage once stood. He managed to get enough clean water to scrub it down and rinse it off. Then he let the sun dry it out. For weeks, as other neighbors tended to their homes, Bobby cared for that couch. When it rained, he put a tarp over it. When the sun was out, he took the opportunity to let it dry out again. The couch that once comforted him was now in his care.

Bobby recalled walking down the middle of his street aimlessly in the days after the storm. Some of the neighbors were rebuilding with the help of family and friends. But unlike Nurse Lindsay's neighborhood, it wasn't a community effort. Bobby had moved here alone. There was nobody local that he was close to. There was also no way for anyone from the outside to get to him. My heart ached as his eyes revealed the isolation that had gripped him in those days.

What Bobby didn't know at the time was that two churches, Christian Life Church and Genesis Church, both from Alabama, had united and sent a team of volunteers to try to help alleviate some of the suffering. They had arrived only three days after the storm, but it took Bobby somewhat longer to find that out. With no car, he learned to walk everywhere. About two weeks after Katrina, Bobby heard that someone was in the K-Mart parking lot with food and clothing and other help.

"They were the first ones to come," he said with such a grateful heart. "I was still walking around a lot, so when I heard they were here, I simply turned and walked in that direction. I walked for miles. I still remember that day. As I got closer, I could smell chicken." He paused, eyes closed, and sniffed the air as if the smell of fresh cooked food still lingered in his nostrils. Tears tried to fill his eyes but he fought them back and swallowed hard and continued. "They brought chicken. I hadn't eaten in eight days!"

Since no words could suffice at that moment, we offered none. He continued, "I remember meeting this man in the parking lot. He was from Minnesota. He asked me if I knew anybody that needed some help and I told him, 'I sure do. Me!' He told me he had a trailer with him and asked if he could park it on my land. Of course I told him he could so he asked me for directions to my address. He said he'd be by later to see what he could do. I didn't think he'd show up. But a few hours later he pulled up with his truck and his trailer and set up camp in my yard." With gratitude evident in every word, the sense of isolation disappeared as Bobby told us how for two weeks straight his new friend would step out of his trailer every morning at 8:00 a.m. sharp, ready for work. No longer alone, Bobby's strength and sense of direction returned. The two labored side by side until the sun and its light gave way, the moon forced them indoors, and their exhausted bodies forced them to rest.

Bobby eventually finished his house. "It's not as grand as it used to be," he said. In fact, his house now occupies the slab where his garage once stood. But it's home. It's his home. In it he can cook his famous pickle-laden potato salad. And at night, you can find him once again in his haven, on his once new, now restored, comfy couch.

Spending time with Bobby was such a blessing. The Lord had heard my plea for a personal connection and arranged this not-so-chance meeting. Still, I wanted more. I didn't want to dismiss the work we had all done that day. Three different homes were being restored. Three different families were being touched. Why was satisfaction so distant for me? On the outside I continued to be an encourager, cheering on the rest of my team and letting them know how much their hard work had blessed me. But I felt in my Spirit that I had still not discovered my purpose. I knew I was there for something or someone special. I also knew I hadn't found them yet. Please don't misunderstand, rebuilding a home for a family is incredible. If you feel you would like to help at all in this awesome and valuable outreach, do it! You will be richly blessed in addition to the families you serve.

But I knew the Lord had sent me for a specific need, and I quietly prayed He would reveal to me just why I was there. About that time, our project manager, Gary, announced, "Something has come up we didn't plan on. We need a roving team to go to another house tomorrow."

I didn't even know what that was. He explained that he had already chosen two people to lay a new tile floor. There was trim work and other odds and ends that needed attention as well. Though none of the folks I had traveled to Mississippi with were going there, I knew I needed to go. When Gary spoke the words, "There is a family living in this house so you'll need to be working while they're there," I felt my heart overflow till it shot right out of the end of my arm, raising my hand to be counted among the roving team members. I had no doubt I needed to be there. I also had no clue that the Lord was about to bless me with a purpose and a week that would never leave me.

Tuesday morning came and still it rained. We gathered for breakfast and set up our tools and teams for the day. We were given the address to our new assignment and Gary showed us the way to the Mercier's home.

One of our younger team members, Josh, who appeared to be auditioning for class clown the night before, was joining a resident volunteer of Camp Katrina to lay a tile floor in one of the bathrooms. While Josh and Brett were restoring the bathroom floor, Josh's father Dan and I worked with three young girls in other parts of the house. We were charged with the task of installing some baseboard trim and other odd jobs.

Gary introduced us to Marvel, the woman of the house, and told us her husband was in "his room" but would be out shortly. While the men were bringing in the heavy equipment like table saws and tile cutters, I got right to work doing what I do best. I plopped down on the couch and started talking to Marvel.

She was shy at first but pleasant. We talked about everything from their storm experience to the fact that she is a cancer survivor. On top of all that, she had been through twenty-two back surgeries, which had left her frustrated and unable to do some of the things she longed to do around the house and in the garden.

We navigated through the first few steps of this newfound friendship carefully at first, each feeling we were to be together, but as yet unsure of where this week would lead. And then I asked her about her children. The floodgate opened! There is something in mothers that creates a universal bond. I learned of her children and grandchildren. I saw pictures of the grandsons together, as well as her granddaughters who'd been born later. One by one I met the family through the precious few photos that had survived Katrina.

I felt almost a bit guilty for not being on the porch where Dan was working. Still, I let the Holy Spirit take control of the conversation, praying as we talked that the Lord would use me to reach this precious woman with His love.

My attention was drawn to a series of paintings on the wall in her living room. There were six separate canvasses that together formed a cross. Each canvas held a portion of Christ's body. It was somewhat modern-art-like, but the message was clearly one of the ages: Christ's crucifixion. Marvel told me her son, Matt, had given it to her and her husband. She explained that not only had it survived Katrina, but it was still hanging in its place on the wall when they returned. It was the only thing that had stayed in place in a home that was completely destroyed by four feet of water flooding in. Surely, we all thought, this was a message from God.

At some point I knew I must rejoin my team and get some work done. Marvel and I kept talking, though, and I cherished the time learning more about her grandchildren and seeing other pieces of Matt's Christ-centered artwork.

After we'd been there an hour or so, Marvel's husband, Elphage, came out of his room to greet us. He apologized for not coming out sooner but explained he had been doing his dialysis. He was a quiet, southern gentleman who seemed unsure of how to re-act to our presence at first. Pride doesn't let a man sit by and watch others take care of his house. Kidney failure doesn't let a man do all the work himself.

Eventually, he took on the foreman's role, showing us all that needed to be done and sharing his vast array of tools. Elphage had obvious experience with these tools, a collection far superior to that of most households. But since dialysis had begun, most of his tools sat abandoned and untouched, collecting dust in boxes and corners of his toolshed.

About midmorning, the girls and I were dutifully measuring and cutting pieces of baseboard trim, and with the help of the pressurized electric nail gun, installing them. As we plugged away, I came to appreciate the gentle way Dan worked with the girls and me. Aware that he could probably finish the job in half the time without us, I was amazed at how patiently he explained each step of the process to us and encouraged us as we learned.

As I sat on the floor struggling to make a corner piece fit, a young police officer stepped in the front door and stood right next to me. Back straight, hands on his hips, he assessed the situation, and us. I jumped to my feet, stuck out my hand and introduced myself. He politely shook my hand, and Marvel explained, "This is one of my sons, Elphage, Jr." From the top of his head to the tips of his spit-polished shoes, his body language screamed skepticism at least, if not downright distrust.

We exchanged niceties, and I continued to engage him, hoping to ease his anxiety about our presence in his parents' home. During the course of our conversation, he mentioned more than once how disgusted he was over his father's situation, but then someone would interject and take the conversation down a different road. Junior would follow and interact, but his mind was still back on his father, his dialysis, and his room.

The next hour and a half was filled with one story after another. As Dan and I stood in a back bedroom with Marvel, Elphage, and Junior, their lives, during and since Katrina, unfolded before us. Elphage and Marvel talked of what it felt like to not have contact with their son for over two weeks, wondering if he and his family had survived. They told us how they rode out the storm in another son's mobile home. They told us of their trip to Dallas with no open gas stations and heavily damaged roads.

They told us of a cousin whose house took on even more water than the four feet that had invaded their home. With two babies to protect, she took an inflatable pool and put them in it. She swam from her house to theirs through debris-infested waters. Evidence of neighbors' lives surrounded her as she swam. Pieces of houses, beds, cars, and other things she refused to imagine, had been engulfed in the storm. She pushed through it all, concentrating only on keeping those babies safe.

Junior talked about his wife and their six-week-old baby riding the storm out on the roof of their house. He told me how she put the baby in a car seat, strapped a life jacket around the seat, and held on to him as Katrina's 180 mph winds pelted them with rain.

He talked about the day before the storm when he and other officers went door- to-door searching for people who had not evacuated. His assignment? To fill out body tags, complete with next of kin, and ask them to wear the tags around their necks.

The day after the storm he had a new assignment: to find bodies, some of which had tags with his handwriting on them, and pull them from the remaining water and up to the street where someone else could collect them.

Aware of the teens who were now listening with us, I asked, "How did you survive this? With everything you've experienced, everything you've seen, how did you get through it all?"

Elphage looked up, thought for a moment, then said, "I guess I'd have to say it was our faith."

At those words, Junior stood up straight, folded his arms, and turned away. It was as if his whole being was rejecting his father's faith. My spirit grieved as I watched the pain and anger take control of this young man. Then those words came back again. "My father's room. No one should be in a room like that. Let alone perform what is supposed to be a sterile procedure. I've tried to get help for him. I even bought the sheetrock he needed but couldn't find anyone to help put it up. As an officer, I was working 20-hour days in the wake of the storm, in addition to rebuilding my own home, which we'd only had for two days when Katrina hit. I did all I could, but I needed help. No one came. I couldn't find anyone to pay any attention to him. It was like he was invisible. He worked as hard as he could to rebuild the house himself, but it's too much for one man. Day after day he toiled alone, unseen."

We were standing right in the middle of a spiritual battle. The enemy's weapons of discouragement and disbelief had pierced his heart. There was internal bleeding. There was only one thing we could do.

"Show me the room." I directed. Confused, he just looked at me. "Show me the room," I repeated. He led the way.

Behind this closed door was the place his father was exiled to four times each day. Elphage had contracted an infection while trying to rebuild his house. With no outside help, too much time passed between the storm and the restoration. The water-logged home became a breeding ground for bacteria. The bacteria attacked Elphage and his kidneys shut down. He was now in renal failure. He was on the transplant list at a New Orleans hospital, but in the meantime, he had to do dialysis four times each day for 30 to 60 minutes each time.

As we peered in the doorway, directly in front of us was his father's chair. An older, leather reclining chair, the type you might expect to see in front of the fireplace or in the midst of the family room. But it sat in isolation. The room was filled to the brim with everything: from his treasured Dallas Cowboys memorabilia to old records and pictures. Even the walls bore remnants of pictures his son had drawn for his grandchildren on a chalkboard-type paper hanging on the upper half of the wall. It also housed several cartons of fluids and equipment for his dialysis.

The lower half of the walls had been destroyed by the floodwaters. In order to salvage what they could, the walls had been cut off at the water line and the entire bottom half was removed down to the studs. The upper walls had been left to protect the family from the outside.

The flooring had been ripped up and removed. Swirls of now-dried mud served as evidence of Katrina's unwelcomed visit.

A small wooden TV tray held his surgical gloves. This was the extent of his sterile environment.

I was horrified and my emotions gathered in my throat as I took in all I was seeing. All I could say was the obvious, "This is unacceptable." As I looked straight into Junior's angry eyes, I realized God was showing me our purpose–in this room, and in his eyes.

"With your permission," I told the family, "I'd like for us to change our focus here. I know you had requested the trim work to be done, but we really need to gut and rebuild this room."

With shocked disbelief Junior said, "You would do that for him?"

"We can't let you continue to live under these conditions." I assured them we would still try to get the other work done, but pleaded with them to let us bring a team in for this new assignment. Elphage smiled ever so slightly and gave us a green light with just a nod of his head.

When we returned to base camp for lunch, I asked, okay, begged, Gary and Pastor Mark, our project leaders, to let us change our focus. Pastor Mark asked Dan and me to share what we had experienced that morning with the rest of the team. The Holy Spirit touched hearts and united us in purpose. There was no budget for this project. There was no prior plan for this. There was also no way we were going to let this opportunity pass us by.

It will probably not surprise you that the Lord had assembled a team designed perfectly to meet the needs of the Mercier family. A painter, a plumber, a pastor, a roofer, and a carpenter were all present. Those with experience in various areas, as well as those with the ability to learn quickly and go beyond their lack of experience, had gathered at that exact moment in time. He had brought us together for His purpose. Armed with a new plan of attack, and our own credit cards, we headed out for the first of many trips to Home Depot and Lowes. We were amazed at how each time we picked up supplies, at least one of the workers there expressed their gratitude "for all you volunteers have done." How did they know? It's not like we had name tags or T-shirts announcing who we were. But time and again we were blessed by people telling us that they could not have survived without the volunteers. Gracious words like, "We can't thank you enough for helping us get our homes and our lives back," were doled out generously and regularly. Keenly aware that some of the men on our team were there for the fifth time, I felt undeserving of their praise, and yet honored to be on this, my first trip to Camp Katrina.

The next few days brought the warrior back, As daunting as this task was, I knew it was for a divine purpose and nothing we encountered could cause that fear to return in me.

By the end of that first day, we could hardly believe the progress at the Mercier's house. Several of us packed up and emptied the room and then ripped down the wallboard from the upper half of the walls. As suspected, the floodwaters from two years previous had wicked up the insulation, creating a breeding ground for black mold and even a couple of lizards. Two of our men donned protective masks and proceeded to rip out the insulation, then bleach and remove the mold in preparation for fresh, new, healthy walls. I wondered if I had ever been like that wall; allowing part of me to be removed due to damage, all the while unaware of the residual, unhealthy organisms still growing in the unsurrendered remnants.

After carefully drying out the room, restoration began. New walls, a hardwood floor, new paint on ceilings and walls. One of our younger women even purchased new miniblinds and curtains for the room.

But the restoration didn't stop there. While during the evening hours at base camp Josh could "yuck it up" with the best of them, on the job he worked harder than anyone ever imagined he could. With very little assistance at first, he continued to tile the bathroom. On his knees and often alone, he was faithful to the task set before him. Any sign of the sometimes tumultuous teen years disappeared, and a sense of pride was restored in his father's heart as together they ministered to this family.

Each day I stood amazed at the team that worked tirelessly and selflessly and the incredible progress they made. A broken roof repaired and shelter restored. A deficient water pump replaced and clean, running water restored. Truckloads of rubble and ruin hauled away and a clean, safe environment restored. A new tile floor installed and a bathroom restored. Every person, every skill, every gift working together in restoration.

We grew close to Elphage and Marvel in that short time. Marvel and I greeted one another each morning, and parted each night with a hug, both grateful for our bond. We prayed for them as Elphage went for a checkup with his doctor and rejoiced with them when they returned with positive news. A newfound strength seemed to fill them as Elphage became more and more involved in the projects we were doing. The men didn't just work for him, they worked with him. Pride and peace were restored in this precious man.

Everyday Junior stopped by to assess our progress. But something was different. Each day his hardened heart seemed to soften a bit. He shared more of his Katrina experience with us, including DVDs he and his friends had taken during and after the storm. On the third day, however, he shared something infinitely more precious; his family. He arrived at the house with his daughter in his arms and his son, the little hurricane survivor, by the hand. Beside him stood a beautiful young woman whose smile lit up the room. I was abundantly blessed that he had taken the time to bring his wife and children to meet us. After talking with us for quite some time, he proudly gave her a tour of his parents' home. The door to his father's room was closed. After they'd seen the rest of the house, I asked if he would like to see how it looked in there. They both nodded and I opened the door to reveal a miracle.

In only three days the room was completely new, right down to the brand new hardwood floor. Every surface was fresh and clean and safe. A smile came across his face as they held hands and stepped into the room. After a brief interchange about all that had been done, I showed him something that to others may have seemed minor. I pulled out the navy blue window valances Sarah had bought. I explained that we picked the color because of his father's love for the Dallas Cowboys. Since we couldn't find actual Dallas Cowboy curtains, we at least wanted them to complement his Cowboy treasures. The room grew silent as tears filled his eyes. They were apparently contagious because his wife and I followed with tears of our own. For several moments we shared in silence. It wasn't just the room. It wasn't all the work. It was the navy blue Dallas Cowboy curtains. Someone had finally seen his Dad–he was no longer invisible.

Exhaustion and excitement intermingled inside me Friday morning. This was our last day. In fact, we only had the morning to work. The team members from Minnesota would continue throughout the afternoon, and a new team would take over once they'd left. But our time together was coming to a close.

Pulling up to the front of the house this last time was vastly different from the first. This home was buzzing with life. Almost every corner of the home and yard hosted busy hands trying to finish what we'd started just four days earlier. Out front was a yard transformed. Since her back surgeries, Marvel's flowerbeds had gone unattended. With two members of our church's landscape ministry present, we couldn't leave without addressing that. So the lawn was cut, and the edges were trimmed. The flowerbeds were relieved of their weeds, and mums restored to their rightful place in Marvel's front yard.

As the worker bees buzzed about in that front yard, you may not have even noticed her at first. Quietly Marvel walked from one side of the yard to another. From the street to the house and back again. After surveying the flowers and drinking in all that she could, she choked back the lump that had filled her throat and said, "I never thought I'd have flowers again. I can't believe you've done this for me." With hugs she thanked Steve, Manny, and Bob who had headed up that project. To this day they can see her face, hear her words, and feel her arms around them. No greater thanks could they have received. Well done, good and faithful servants.

Noontime came way too soon. We knew it was time to say good-bye. Marvel and I held each other tight, not wanting to let our time together end. Hands were shaken, thank-yous and good-byes exchanged. Then a voice of wisdom said, "We're going to pray."

Immediately we joined hands with Marvel and Elphage and prayed for them. Genuinely grateful for our time there, we thanked God for allowing us this privilege. As I began to close in prayer, Elphage spoke up. "I want to pray, too." With a few deep breaths to strengthen him, he thanked God for all that had been done and for sending us to them. We held hands in silence as he collected himself for his closing words. Then, Elphage whispered the phrase that defined our week. "And thank you for restoring our faith."

I am so grateful to have been part of the team that week. The Lord taught me an important lesson about spiritual warfare and the weapons used. In this violent and volatile world there are some who fight in the name of their god. We see them all too often on the evening news. But spiritual warfare is for one purpose and one purpose only: Restoration. It is to restore us to a life with Him.

You see, the weapons God would have us use do not kill and wound. Instead they preserve life and heal. They do not destroy homes and lives. Instead, they restore them. His weapons are not purchased in gun shops or on black markets, or even purchased at all, for that matter. They are given, freely. They are not put in the hands of violent hearts, but in the hands of those whose hearts are bowed in prayer.

I witnessed spiritual warfare, and victory, that week. In victory I witnessed Restoration. Restoration wrought by new spiritual weapons. New to me, not Him. For I witnessed hammers and nails putting things back into their rightful place. I witnessed screw guns and sheetrock rebuilding walls—not the kind that keep us from each other or exclude others, but walls that protect families from life's storms. I witnessed people's lives insulated from the cold world outside. And I witnessed new life growing from a simple bunch of maroon-colored mums planted in a freshly-weeded flowerbed.

Restoration, as defined by Webster, is "the act of restoring something or someone to a satisfactory state." But apparently God does not look to Webster to define His Restoration. God never stops at "satisfactory." For as I saw in Waveland, whether in your home, or in your heart, God's Restoration is always Glorious!

I don't want to go through the motions.
I don't want to face one more day.
Without your all consuming passion inside of me.
I don't want to spend my whole life asking,
"What if I had given everything
instead of going through the motions?"

"The Motions" – Matthew West

5

A NEW CHALLENGE

In 2007 we faced a new challenge, a need we could not ignore. A young boy named Foday was brought to Dennis at the orphanage. His head, arms, and legs bore the scars of a brutal attack from the war. His eyes bore the pain that continued from both the memory, and the life lived since as a disfigured child. I will share his story, without editing, in his own words. Please be warned, they paint a very honest but graphic picture of his experience.

"Sadly enough when the rebels attacked the village and hunted young men and children like us, most of us went and hid ourselves. When the rebels didn't get the young men they wanted, they went in search of us in the bush, and I was caught together with my two sisters who were instantly raped, and as soon as my parents heard the voices of my sisters when crying they went out of the bush and 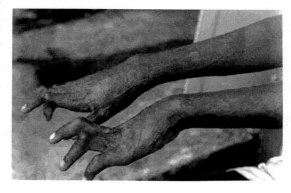 screamed, 'stop raping my daughters,' and immediately one of the rebels took the arm and shot my mom and dad. Instantly we started crying; they asked us to choose whether we wished to be killed or not crying for our parents. As soon as my sisters heard that they stopped crying, but I continued to cry so the commander asked one of his boys to set fire on me. Instantly they put the petrol on my feet, hands and head and lit fire on me. When they moved on, an old man came out of the bush and started throwing water on me."

♡

I don't think anyone could know just how deep his scars went. I still cry when I see pictures of him, like the one on the previous page. I wasn't sure how, but I knew we had to help. I knew it would take much more financial support than anything I'd ever imagined. I also knew God would provide much more than I'd ever dreamed.

It was during this time that I was contacted by a man I'll call Christopher. He is a friend of a family member. If I recall, he heard me speak at one of the churches I'd worked with. He said he was having a meeting with several key managers of his company. He explained that about twenty-five people would be flying in from around the world and, though it was somewhat short notice, he'd like to know if I could come speak to the group. He told me how they had discussed being more involved in philanthropic efforts, and wanted me to share what we were doing through Hearts In Action. Incredible!

It's funny, as I look back on that day, I remember things almost in small snap shots. I picture myself following Christopher up the stairs, wondering if he could see how nervous I was. After all, Foday was counting on me. Support from a group like this could change his life. I couldn't blow it. I needed to give the performance of a lifetime, Foday's lifetime.

Everything went very well. I had a small presentation prepared, but just tried to talk from my heart. I sensed they had seen the need. I felt many of them were following with me as I described the journey that had brought me to that point. Questions were batted about as they brainstormed together. Some questions were directed to me, but many were just thrown out there to hang above the 25-foot-long mahogany conference room table. It was exciting. It was terrifying. It was right where I wanted to be.

As the questioning began to slow, a gentleman at the exact opposite end of the conference table caught my eye. He said he needed to ask me a very important question. The room grew eerily silent as all eyes were on him. It was obvious this was a man of great stature within this company. I took a deep breath and whispered a little prayer for the right answer. I imagined a huge celebration as the right answer lingered in the air and all the participants simultaneously erupted in applause and support. That was, however, only imagined. His next question stunned me into a moment of silence. His words were soft, but forceful. "I notice," he said, "that you often refer to 'the Lord' or 'God' when you are talking about this project. I'm just wondering if you'd be comfortable leaving that language out. If you'd be satisfied with talking about the humanitarian effort, but not referring to God."

We all sat for just a second or two without so much as breathing. I knew what hung in the balance, and it wasn't money. The words of Matthew swirled through my head. "If you deny me before men, I will deny you before my Father in heaven." The very core of who and why I am was at stake. I was fully aware of where this was heading and what he would likely say or do depending on my answer. I knew that one compromise on my part could seal the deal. I also knew that compromise was not something I could live with.

"I understand your concern from a corporate perspective," I replied gently after clearing my throat. "But I truly believe it was God who called me to do this. I believe it is the Lord who has provided all that we have needed, right up to and including this meeting today. I cannot deny Him or exclude Him, or I would not be true to who He has called me to be. I recognize that may not be something you can live with, and if that's the case, I'm sorry. But it is the way I must go, regardless of whether or not you'll come along."

Please don't think I'm brave for saying that. I am not. But I had absolutely no other choice. I had walked in there with the idea that everything was resting on my shoulders. As I spoke those words to him, God was speaking to me as well. Who was I trusting? Was I trusting in me? In my ability to share the story in such a way that they could not resist helping? Was I trusting in the people that filled the room? In their money? The Lord has always provided all that we needed. With Him all things are possible. I drove home more determined than ever, even knowing I would never hear from them again.

Over the next few months I spent hours on the phone trying to solidify the arrangements for Foday to come to the United States for his much needed medical care. I contacted Shriner's Hospital for Children in Boston, Massachusetts. This particular location specializes in caring for burn victims. I explained Foday's situation, sent them pictures, filled out forms, and had conference calls, until they determined that they thought they would be able to help him, despite the number of years over which the scarring had taken place. We were ecstatic!

There was so much to do now that we had the surgeons in place. The coordinator at the hospital told me that Foday would have to be here as much as four or five months. We would need housing, food, transportation, and possibly a host family to help with all of the above. We launched a fund-raising project called "30 in 30." We needed to raise $30,000 in 30 days.

My career within the insurance industry had blossomed at the same time as Hearts In Action was growing. I had met so many interesting people. I had risen through the ranks and spent time as a corporate sales trainer, during which time I met a lovely woman named Marilena. She was such a beauty! She and I loved spending time together in and out of work, though I suspected we came from two very different worlds. I shared with her all the stories of our mission and what I was trying to accomplish. When I spoke of Foday's predicament, she asked me to send her all the information I could about him and what we were trying to accomplish. I did that, secretly hoping she might make a donation. Thankfully God sees beyond our hopes and gives us our dreams. Marilena connected me with someone close to her who, after an extensive conference call and many questions, pledged to give whatever amount we needed to reach our goal in that 30 days, no limits. No matter what, we would have the funds we needed to get Foday here.

Within 30 days everything was in place. The funding, of course, was raised. We had volunteers lined up for host families. We had transportation to and from the hospital in the works. We even had an airline that donated the round trip airfare. Only one thing remained, getting Foday a Visa so he could leave his country for ours to get the help he so desperately needed.

Over the months that we had been planning, my husband had researched what we needed to get the Visa approved. It is not an easy process, to say the least. There was the application, of course, but it didn't end there. We also had to provide documentation that everything was taken care of, including letters from the hospital stating they were providing the care for free, and letters from Hearts In Action stating we had raised the funds necessary to allow him to stay for four to five months without being a drag on the US government. It was a lot of work but we gathered it all and faxed it to the embassy in Sierra Leone and anxiously awaited the news that his Visa was ready. We had done all we could. In just over two weeks we would finally meet Foday face to face at Logan International Airport. Dennis and Foday checked daily with the embassy, while my husband and our family headed out for a week's vacation on Cape Cod to rest up in anticipation of the busy months ahead.

It was Wednesday, exactly one week before the big arrival. My husband and I sat peacefully on the back deck with my brother- and sister-in-law. Each morning we met there to talk and enjoy watching pairs of gorgeous, white birds gracefully floating on the water aptly named Swan Pond. I thought, "This must be one of the most relaxing places on earth." Trees and flowers, meticulously cared for by the home's owner, surrounded the second floor deck. A stone path along the edge of a blanket of lush green lawn not often found on the Cape spanned the space below. Off to the left side of the yard a path led to the water. Kayaks and an inflatable boat waited every morning, calling out for us to enjoy them. But the deck won out. A cup of Tetley, a good book, and great friends held us there, content to be still and let the swans entertain us with their synchronized swimming.

That morning, the alarming sound of my cell phone interrupted our quiet. The number was from Sierra Leone. "Hey Dennis," I shouted with the biggest smile I could find. I knew he was scheduled to be at the Embassy that morning with Foday and assumed he was calling to tell me that the Visa was ready and they were all set to travel the following week. I couldn't have been more wrong. He and Foday were at the embassy and were told Foday had been denied his Visa. He begged me to call and talk to the person in charge. Foday sobbed in the background as he told Dennis, "I thought I was finally going to have my healing." My heart sunk so low it shattered on the floor.

I hung up the phone in utter disbelief. After all of these months, how could this be? We had jumped through every hoop they asked us to. We had taken care of every detail they could think of. We had raised every dollar needed, and still they were denying him what could very well be his best and only opportunity to return some sense of normalcy to his life.

Months earlier I had spoken to Foday on the phone. It was not easy because he spoke very little English, but our hearts had spoken to each other despite our ears not understanding every word. He told me he had spent a lot of time sitting off in the distance, watching other people, because others were afraid of him and the way he looks. He told me he hoped that children would play with him now and that people would not think he was so odd. He was hopeful for a future far different from his past. I promised we would do what we needed to get him here. I looked forward to a handshake, or better yet a hug, from a boy who had grown up so far away yet lived so close to my heart.

I promised. And now he stood in the middle of Siaka Stevens Street in one of the poorest nations in the world, his broken dreams flowing down his face as he cried out for the loss of something he almost had.

I called out to the deck to Kevin and told him what was going on. Our minds were reeling. Outrage and frustration replaced the peace of just a few minutes ago. We began strategizing, trying to figure this out. Surely this is just some kind of a mistake. At first we thought it was the US that was denying him entrance. We started making phone calls, looking up emails and contacts in a desperate attempt to correct this crazy outcome. I even called the offices of some of the men running for President, appealing to either their humanity, or their desire to win; either would do if they would help.

We spent hours trying to find someone with the power to make this happen. I felt desperation rising in my chest. I felt trapped somewhere between bursting out in tears and screaming out in frustration. Finally, my husband was able to get a man from the consulate in Sierra Leone on the phone. Shocking as it may seem, it wasn't the United States that was denying him access. It was Sierra Leone denying him the chance to leave! Kevin could hardly believe his ears. Why would a country stop a young man who had been severely injured from getting the medical care he needed? Why would they refuse the gift the hospital, doctors, volunteers, donors, and airlines had all given this young life? Why?

In one last futile attempt to reach this man, Kevin spoke up and asked, "Have you seen this boy?!" Surely you could not forget a seventeen year old who is bald down the middle of his head, has scar tissue on his legs and feet, and whose hands are contracted due a senseless, vicious attack. "Have you seen this boy?" he repeated.

"Have you seen this country?" was the response. "This country is so poor, so desolate, so terrible that if we let him leave, he will not come back."

"But we will be responsible for taking care of him. We will make sure he comes back as soon as the surgeries have been completed," Kevin begged.

"As I said, this is a horrible place. He will not come back. We will not let him go."

Just like that. It was over. The door not only shut, it slammed in Foday's face, with the force of the blow felt on two continents.

In the year or two that followed, we pursued other avenues. I remembered a floating hospital called Mercy Ships that travels from port to port, country to country, providing much needed medical care and surgery as they go. I was able to make arrangements for them to care for Foday. The ship was docking in Liberia. As long as we could get him there, they would see him for an evaluation and could do the surgery right there on the ship.

Dennis and Foday arrived in Liberia on a Thursday. We had sent them a camera so Dennis could document the progress and the trip for our donors. On Friday, Foday was checked in and given a bed on the ship. I spoke to a nurse on the ship who said he was safe and sound and resting. This was good news. Liberia is a dangerous country and the area they had to travel through was filled with violence. It was a relief to know they had arrived safely.

The relief, however, was short-lived. While Foday rested, Dennis went out to take care of some business. We had only sent him with enough money to get there. We did not want to endanger him by having him carry a lot of money on his way. He headed for the Western Union office to pick up some additional cash now that they were settled in. We transferred the money, Dennis collected it and left for the room he was staying in. As he walked, he was approached by several men who had seen him coming out of the Western Union office. Before he knew it they had jumped him and stolen the camera and all of the money. We were, of course, thankful they didn't hurt him. He is an incredible man with an enormous heart for the children. Money can be replaced, cameras too, but not him.

The weekend passed with no word from Dennis. I still don't know how he survived without any money for food. On Monday, the evaluations began. People of all ages had been brought, walked, or crawled to get medical attention not normally available. At the end of the day, the doctors told Dennis they were not going to be able to help Foday. Another crushing blow.

I began calling the ship to find out what the problem was. It was like a nightmare that comes back to haunt you again and again. I was able to speak to one of the doctors who was obviously bothered by the decision to turn Foday away. However, he said that over 3,000 people showed up that day for help. They had to triage those people and decide who would benefit the most from their help. Since Foday's injuries were now almost a decade old, and not an imminent danger, he fell to the bottom of the list. The doctor also shared something I had not known until then. He told me Foday was developmentally challenged as well. "Even if we were able to do the surgery," he said, "Foday probably would not have been able to withstand the months of physical therapy he would need to keep the fingers from contracting again." There was also some doubt anyone would be available in Kamasassa Village, or anywhere close for that matter, to oversee the therapy. I told him I understood. And I did, intellectually. I just couldn't convince my heart to understand.

Dennis called me back to see what I had been able to arrange. I told him what I knew and that he would just have to head back home without the surgery. I made another Western Union transfer that was enough to buy plane tickets back. I didn't want them to travel that road again. I just wanted them safely back home. Bitter tears streamed through the dust on Foday's face as he set out for the orphanage, defeated and beaten down by the deafening sound of another slamming door.

I wish I could tell you that at some future point we were able to get Foday's surgery completed. I wish I could tell you that he was healed, inside and out, that everything we ever set out to do ends in a "Happily Ever After." But that's only in the movies. There has been so much we have done, and will continue to do. But this, I have to admit, is one of my deepest regrets. Perhaps someday my heart will understand, too.

♡

As we worked together throughout the years, Dennis' family continued to grow. When we first started working with him he was married and had a son. A year or so later he and his wife were blessed with a second child, a baby girl. When he sent me the information about her being born, height, weight, and so on, I noticed one thing was missing. A name. He explained to me that they do not give their child a name until he or she is eight days old. I am not sure of the exact reason for that, but in a region where twenty percent of babies do not survive those eight days, I can guess.

At the end of the eight days he emailed me that she was doing well and they were ready to name her. He asked me if I would mind if they named her "Natalie." Would I mind? He must have been kidding. Not only would I not mind, I would be honored. I cannot think of any other word sufficient to describe my feelings. Honored.

There was a ceremony to celebrate naming her. It is their custom to have the person the baby is being named after hold the baby during the ceremony. They invited to me to come, but it is very difficult to secure safe travel in Sierra Leone. I wanted so much to attend, but just couldn't make it happen. So, her grandmother stood in for me. Dennis sent me a picture of his mother and daughter. I cherish it to this day.

We entered into a blessed partnership, and friendship, with Dennis in 2004. We continued working with him for close to seven years. During that time we saw ups and downs, tragedies and triumphs. We fed, clothed, and cared for seventeen children and showed them the love of Christ through those who worked there. We were able to give small salaries to the women who cared for and cooked for the children, enabling them to feed their families as well. The money that had been donated for Foday's surgery fed the children for many months to come, with the blessing of the donors, of course.

In 2009 we faced another challenge. In all the prior years, Dennis was soft and kind and very diligent about receipts and documentation for donations. In fact, there were times he told me to hold a donation until he could send the receipts for the previous month. But something in his "voice" began to change early in 2009. It's hard to explain, since we only had contact through email at this point. His phone calls had stopped. I grew concerned about the tone and urgency with which the emails were sent. I began contacting other agencies to try to find someone who could provide safe guides for us to travel there to inspect the work that was being done and see if Dennis was okay. In the past I had always been able to have a third party check on things, but now I was finding many organizations pulling out of the country. I was no longer able to contact the same people. I prayed earnestly about how to handle the situation I was facing.

About mid-year I asked the Lord to very clearly open and shut doors as needed. The "voice" in the emails did not seem like my friend, Dennis, any longer. Still, with the lives of seventeen children in the balance, I could not just cut him off. I asked questions of him that only Dennis would know the answer to. I was not completely satisfied with all of the answers. I continued to pray for wisdom. In retrospect I think the Holy Spirit was giving that to me as I, sometimes trusting to a fault, grew more and more wary of the person on the other end of the emails.

Finally, in November I cried out one more time, almost in agony, "Lord, shut the door if this is not Dennis anymore." One last email came through demanding we send money right away or they were going to have to shut the orphanage down. He told us that the government had inspected them and told them they would be shut down if they didn't fix some things. He said that if we didn't send money right away he would have to send the children to foster care. This time my husband contacted the Ministry of Social Welfare, Gender and Children's Affairs directly and inquired about this mandate. The gentleman on the other end of the phone said he was unaware of any outstanding directives for our orphanage. He then stated that he would highly doubt it to be true as the conditions in most of their orphanages are so terrible that he couldn't imagine the government shutting one down because the kitchen sink wasn't working properly. That was it. The last door had closed.

I returned the email I had received with our regrets. I told the sender there would be no money and to go ahead and send the children to foster care. Then I cried.

I realize this is another "less than fairy tale ending." I suppose I could have made it sound "rosy" by talking about the children going to foster care, but I believe that if you are to trust me, transparency is needed, even when the outcome isn't what we would have liked.

I don't know if I'll ever know the whole story of what happened there. I don't know if I'll ever hear from Dennis again. But I do know, without a doubt, that Dennis was a good and faithful servant. I do know, without a doubt, that what we did for more than seven years was significant, life-changing, "Love Through Me" work. I can only pray that my dear friend from the other side of the world is safe. We may never cross paths again on this side of eternity, but maybe on the next.

Having had this tremendous experience in Sierra Leone, I was more determined than ever to work in missions. However, my husband and I agreed that we would only work in an area we could travel to. It is imperative to ensure our donors' money is going where it was intended and being used for what it was intended for.

Plus, the Lord has so strongly put missions on my heart and the desire to be on the ground, on the front lines, working with the children and the caregivers directly. I need to allow the Lord to touch others through me so they will know His love in a tangible way. Little did I know that just one month later, in January, 2010, an earthquake on a tropical island would bring that all to be.

I wanna live like that and give it all I have,

So that everything I say and do points to you.

If love is who I am, then this is where I stand,

Recklessly abandoned, never holding back.

I wanna live like that.

"Live Like That" — Sidewalk Prophets

6

HAITI, OH MY HAITI

The Balcony

I stand on this balcony today, likely for the last time, no longer shocked but still moved and overwhelmed by what I see. Straight ahead is a hillside strewn with piles of concrete, remnants of homes that once were. Some have retained just enough of their original shape to be recognized for what they used to be. Rebar[2] pushes through the rubble everywhere as if it doesn't realize it's no longer doing its job. Scattered in, around, and atop of these piles are playing children. I know, I know, it's too dangerous for children. But this is not only where they play, it is their home.

One building, in the center of the hill, managed not to collapse completely. Crumbled at one corner and sagging on one side, still the roof of this house, a slab of compromised concrete is the playground for two of the children. They are there most every day. I can't always see them well enough to know what they're playing, but I gasp each time one of them wanders close to the unguarded edge.

---

[2] A rebar (short for reinforcing bar), also known as reinforcing steel, is a steel bar, commonly used as a tensioning device in reinforced concrete and reinforced masonry structures holding the concrete in compression.

Glancing just to my right I see tents. So many tents. And shelters made of pieces of plastic, cloth, metal, even cardboard for those families not lucky enough to have received one of the millions of tents distributed right after the earthquake. But that was back when the world was still paying attention. As with all of the tent cities in Port-au-Prince, the condition of the shelters varies greatly. The harsh heat and tropical storms that have passed over have shredded much of the canvas. The cloth coverings provide a bit of shelter from the scorching afternoon sun, but none of them, as I learned this week, can keep out the sludge that runs to and fro, washing mud and waste over and through the places people live in.

Separating the rubble from the tents is a dirt road. It is rutted deeply, partially from the serious shaking it received, and partially from the rivers that run down the hill, which come from the evening rains.

Directly in front of me another dirt road lines the other side of the hotel wall. Like most Haitian city streets, garbage of every kind flanks the road on both sides. This one has an especially large mound leaning against the outside of the hotel wall. Children run through and climb up this rotting, fly ridden pile. To my knowledge, there have been no attempts to clean it up. That is, except for the hogs that roam throughout the city, eating all they can from the slimy slop. Apparently, sticking their snouts deep in the mush somehow keeps the stench from permeating their brains. In the United States we argue we should eat only grass-fed cattle in fear of what food sources will transmit through the meat to us. In Haiti the luckiest children have someone who will share the unwashed machete-slaughtered animals now grazing in this pile.

At night my eyes and ears seem to experience two different worlds. As I look out past the wall, all I can see is darkness. Complete, utter darkness. But I hear the voices of thousands talking, laughing, living there. It is confusing as my senses seem to contradict each other. I can hear them. I can smell the fires burning (campfires, I hope). I know they are there. But my eyes will not assist me once the sun is gone. All I can do is listen. I need to be quiet, and listen.

I remember the first time I saw this balcony. It had been a long, hot, exhausting day. I had survived the flight, walking from the airport to our bus with a seriously overweight suitcase, hauling that suitcase from the bus, up the stairs of the hotel, around the back and to the base of a three-story wrought iron spiral staircase. Where were the bellhops? Where were the elevators? The balcony beckoned me to come on up, but I wasn't sure I could. I watched the others hike up the twists and turns with excitement. I couldn't very well ask another woman for help, so I put one foot in front of the other and dragged my suitcase up all three flights. I may not be strong, but I am tenacious. Besides, "I can do all things through Christ who strengthens me"[3] (including making it up those stairs).

From the moment I first stood on this balcony out-side my room, it has been my friend. Its solid cement floor has held me up high above the wall so that I can continue to watch the world around me. It served as a meeting place from time to time as I met friends on their way in or out of their rooms. Mostly, though, it just held me, day after day, as I sat processing all I had experi-

---

[3] Philippians 4:13

enced–allowing me to sit in my quiet and write in my journal so that I could share my story with you.

In the pages that follow you will find that story. I pray you are moved, blessed, and maybe even challenged, as we travel this week together.

Arrival

A staggering statistic: in Haiti there is a 40 percent death rate for children ages zero to four.

Sunday October 3, 2010

Spirit Airlines delivers us to our destination. We will stay in Ft. Lauderdale tonight, then on to Haiti in the morning. It seems incredible that we are finally on our way. In January an earthquake hit the country of Haiti, and I felt led to go as soon as possible. I never dreamed that it would take 9 months to get there!

There are 19 people altogether on this trip. I am traveling with a group from Christ Church in East Greenwich, Rhode Island. We are all different ages, shapes and sizes, backgrounds and gifts united for one purpose: to serve Him by serving others. How that will play out exactly, we do not know. Some are hoping for building projects. Some are hoping for Vacation Bible School. I am hoping for both time in a clinic or hospital and time in an orphanage. But what I want most is to make a difference in someone's life. I pray for a powerful ministry while I am here. I have found that if you just re-main open to His leading, He will guide you to where you should be. My own preconceived ideas of what would be best will undoubtedly pale in comparison to where He will lead. My trip to Mississippi a few years ago proved that. So, I wait with wonder and awe at what this week will bring.

I will say this, if the chaos and challenges we faced in our family over the last couple of weeks are any indication, Satan must be about to lose some ground in Haiti. I admit I didn't recognize the battle going on at first, but this morning it came to me as I prayed about the past week. What a clear example of the enemy trying to throw us off track! And yet, I am filled with His peace! The peace that passes all understanding. I can almost not believe it myself! God is so good! He is victorious! He will use us this week in a mighty way. Lord, let me hear your call and be faithful to your purpose for me. Amen.

Monday, October 4, 2010

With very little sleep only our excitement is fueling us as we sit on the plane that will take us to our mission. We've filled out our customs paperwork and anxiously await that feeling in our stomachs signaling the beginning of our descent into Port-au-Prince. Lord, prepare us— should I say *continue* to prepare us?—for the people you will reach through us in the next few days. Thank you, thank you, thank you for this opportunity. Amen.

Pastor Noel and Pastor Stan met us at the airport. Pastor Noel, a Haitian, was our local guide for the week. Pastor Stan, who works with Discovery Mission, was there to shepherd us through this mission experience. His years of experience leading short-term missions was evident from the very moment we met him. He knew how to guide us through the system and advise us on what we would experience. He watched vigilantly over each of us and maneuvered each detail of the week with grace. He was strong, but patient. Most of all, the abundance of the fruit he displayed bore witness to a man full of the Holy Spirit. Throughout the week I saw the

Lord pour out strength, grace, and wisdom through him. He amazed me time and again as he seemed to have a window into each of us, understanding and therefore guiding us based on what the Lord was doing in us individually, not just as a group. One of his greatest gifts (totally opposite of mine) is his silence. Sometimes I'd pour my heart out about something that had happened that day, and he listened–carefully–and then smiled. That's it. He just smiled. Not necessarily giving me his opinion, but instead let me sit and ponder, praying for the Holy Spirit's leading. That's not to say he didn't guide us, he did. He just didn't spoon-feed us answers. Once I laughed and told him at times I wanted to scream and ask him what he was thinking. He, of course, just smiled.

Another person, Jim, joined our leadership team. Jim pitched in anywhere there was a need. But the thing I appreciated most about him was his incredible talent with photography. Every day he created a beautiful slide show set to music. We're all familiar with the saying, "A picture paints a thousand words." For Jim, an entire novel unfolded with one slide show. Each night after dinner we gathered around his laptop and relived the day.

As we exited the airport and headed for our bus, I was overcome by the intense heat. I was dragging a large suitcase behind me, wishing I had just brought a little backpack. The suitcase not only had my clothing, but also tons of candy, granola bars, and even envelopes of tuna. The candy and granola bars were to give to the children. The tuna, however, was my safety net in case the food we were served had the potential for bothering my stomach.

Why is it I can change wound dressings, change diapers, wipe noses with my bare hand, and even kiss the dirty little feet of a Haitian baby, but the thought of new and different foods frightens me? How weird.

We climbed into the bus and began the ride to the hotel. I don't believe it was very far, although I'm not sure because we seemed to take many different routes throughout the week. Vehicles of every size and shape filled the streets. We learned two things very quickly: first, no matter how wide, or narrow, a street is, there are no actual lanes. No dotted lines, no solid lines, no lanes at all. You can pass anywhere you feel brave enough to do so, despite oncoming traffic. And, second, apparently whoever honks the loudest, or the longest, gets his way! For the most part, being in a full-sized bus gave us an advantage as our driver thought nothing of pulling out into oncoming traffic as long as they were smaller than us. The only other vehicles that seemed better equipped were the tiny motorcycle "taxis." The road, the sidewalk, in between the cars–it seemed there was no path they would not try. After all, they had horns, too!

When we finally got to our hotel, it was a bit of an oasis. By US standards, it rivals a Motel 6 except it had undrinkable water and an outdoor spiral wrought iron staircase to the third floor. For Haiti, it was luxury. From 6:30 p.m. to 6:30 a.m. our rooms were air conditioned. In the center of the complex was a large patio area and a pool. When we first arrived, some of our team members were complaining that we weren't staying in the field with the children. After just one day in Haiti, I was personally so very thankful for the blessings that brought relief from the heat.

Monday, October 4

We had a good day of getting to know each other today. There are three people that arrived throughout the day from other states. They have joined us in our mission. I pray we will fully welcome them into our team.

For a while we played some games in a circle, laughing and breaking the ice. Then we got down to business as we shared our reasons for being here and what we hope to accomplish this week. The answers, like the people, are varied. But there is a common thread of a desire to help others and serve our Lord.

At dinner, Stan announced our assignment: New Life Children's Home. That's where we are headed tomorrow. It is a rescue orphanage. After dinner, Stan and I talked a bit about one of the children there. I cannot remember how the conversation started. I may have told him I wanted to work with some of the handicapped children. God may have told him that. Whatever the case, he began sharing with me a little about Valerie. He explained that, for her own safety, she needed to be restrained by her wrists and ankles at all times. I found this both intimidating and personally challenging. I say personally because I have read studies about the difference human touch can make. Why did I even know that? It must have been for her. I told Stan I'd like to try to work with her. Somehow his eyes revealed he already knew that.

So tomorrow we will head to work at the orphanage. Lord, let us be a blessing!

New Life Children's Home

"In Haiti people either push, pull, or carry for a living. Where does that leave a child who is disabled?" –Miriam Frederick

In 1977, Miriam Frederick came to Haiti for the first time. She has stayed for more than three decades. In that time she has used her passion for children, her training in nursing, and her faith in Jesus Christ to serve the poorest of the poor. Periodically Miriam leads teams of volunteers into the mountainous regions of Haiti. These areas have virtually no other source of medical care. Local doctors do the best they can, but are seriously understaffed, underfunded, and understocked. Miriam's teams are a welcome sight as they bring much-needed medicine and help to these beleaguered people.

Hundreds travel, for hours and even days, over mountains and through rugged terrain to be seen in one of these clinics. Parents bring their sick children, many on the verge of dying, in hopes of finding help and healing. Each time, there are children for whom doctors determine their only hope for healing will be found by taking them to the city for extensive medical care. Sometimes the decision as to whom they can bring back is excruciating. They face limited re-

sources for an unlimited need. Ultimately, Miriam has to decide who returns with them, and who she will pray will make it until her next visit.

The children that have been rescued are now part of New Life Children's Home (NLCH), in Port-au-Prince. This is home base for the ministry. Currently they care for more than 150 formerly rescued children. So many of them run and play and learn and grow. Obvious to the naked eye is the physical healing that has taken place for each of them. Just as obvious is the spiritual and emotional healing they've experienced as well. Despite what you might imagine, it is a happy place.

When we entered the gates of NLCH, we were greeted by the customary conflicting sights of Haiti. At the gate, for instance, is a young man dressed in jeans and a T-shirt and armed with a rifle. For me this is an unusual and, at first, unsettling sight. His face is not friendly, nor is it meant to be, for he guards the tranquility of this place.

Glancing a few hundred feet beyond him, we beheld a harbor of safety in a sea of despair. A huge mango tree grows in the front, center of the yard, a sign of rest, a sign of relief, a sign of life.

The dirt road splits in two at that mango tree, into two semicircles that border a lush green lawn, at least by Haiti's standards. Turn to the right and it will take you to the fish hatchery, rabbit cages, and vegetable garden. Turn to the left and it will take you by the main building, past the guesthouse, a small building with two showers, and eventually to the area where the children play and eat and sleep. Both roads end there, leading visitors to the heart of the ministry, at the base of another mango tree.

Upon arrival, we jumped off the bus and headed left, to the main building, where we met Miriam Frederick.

We had awakened early that morning in anticipation of meeting the children. First we had to have our breakfast at the hotel, then load ourselves and our supplies onto the bus, travel through the crazy traffic of the city to the orphanage. We bounded off the bus and our excitement rose as we heard the children in the distance. Still we had to wait. Stan and Jim had to give us instructions, "rules of engagement" if you will. We also had to wait for Miriam to be ready to greet us. After sharing a little history of the ministry with us, Miriam told us of all the things she needed help with that week. We had our work cut out for us because she had quite a list! Just to start, there were walls to paint, screens to fix, a piece of land to clear, and a foundation for a new building to build. There were supplies to sort, a trailer to unload, and school backpacks to fill. But first we needed to meet the children for whom we were toiling.

The long-awaited tour began. It all seemed so surreal. We had waited for this moment. Finally, we stood facing the open air building, a kind of pavilion, filled with children of all ages. The building had a roof and walls on each side about waist high that sat on a concrete platform, and there were tables spaced throughout. The children's "teacher" was with them and as we all filed into place, he directed them to welcome us. Beautiful voices filled the air as they welcomed us in song. After singing two or three songs, on cue they all came out to greet us. The younger ones ran into any open arms. We were mutually blessed in embrace. The older children expressed a variety of emotions. Some, like the younger ones, gave an enthusiastic hug. Some shook your hand politely and greeted you with "Bonjour[4]." Some simply leaned in as if allowing you to reach out your arms to envelop them, but it was not reciprocated.

During the few moments we were engaged in this greeting ritual, I felt conflicted. I couldn't help but wonder if some of the older children felt they were on display. Yet, I understood the need, for their sakes as well as ours, for them to interact with us. This turned out to be a bit of a dilemma for me throughout the week. So many times I wanted to linger by the scenes that bombarded my senses. At the same time, I didn't want anyone to feel like their suffering was the subject of our entertainment. How do you fully take in all that you see, hear, and smell, and still respect the privacy of someone living in the open on the side of the street?

As the children continued to move among us, a young girl named Mitaille came into view: Mitaille made her way through the crowd with her arms held tightly by her sides. Her hands were clenched inward, obviously not available to touch. Dutifully she navigated this obstacle course with eyes turned downward. While others continued to enjoy the interaction with the children, my gaze was fixed on her. She passed close by me and I somehow caught her eye. Still nothing. No smile. No greeting. Just a passerby.

---

[4] Bonjour is French for "good day" or "hello."

About an hour later I was talking to someone about the work we had ahead of us. I believe it was washing down walls and painting. But I was distracted by the feeling I was being watched. I looked around and saw Mitaille standing about 50 feet away. She had lifted her eyes to search for mine. I smiled. She didn't. We both moved on.

Over the next few hours our undeclared game of hide-and-seek continued. With each round, the distance between us closed. All around us children were playing with my friends. There was so much joy and laughter! Soccer balls, swings, seesaws–all being put to good use. But Mitaille and I continued our quiet chess-like maneuvers, each wondering what the other's next move would be.

I sat on a bench on the edge of the playground and took it all in. I was witnessing memories being made. I was also learning. I learned something simple from one of our team members, Chris. He would sit on the stairs, or a bench, or anywhere that had a little room next to him. He'd smile and pat the seat next to him in invitation to a waiting child. Somehow that little pat served as interpreter for the child and said, "It's okay. You can sit here. I welcome you in." Never did the invitation meet with resistance.

So as I sat on the bench with Rick and a little boy, I tried it. Mitaille had moved in a little closer. Our eyes were locked as only a sidewalk stood between us. I scooted to my right and patted my hand on the empty space now available to my left. Four or five steps later she stood right in front of me. After carefully evaluating the situation, she turned and sat down, but not on the bench. She sat directly on my lap. Careful to match her pace, I gently touched her arm, controlling my own desire to wrap her in a hug.

Over the next hour or so we silently grew closer. She held my hand tightly, the way you would hold onto something you don't want to lose. She led me around the yard, exploring and discovering tiny beads that had been dropped during a previous craft time. She loved her beads. Something so simple, something so significant. As she showed me each one, I remarked on its beautiful color. Then she led me to another corner of the playground.

Though language was still a barrier, we had made small breakthroughs. Wherever we went, she turned her back to me, grabbed both of my hands, and wrapped my arms around her in a tight embrace. She kept that grip so tight it was hard to walk without tripping over her.

At one point, I motioned toward the swing set. Hand in hand we headed past the seesaws where giggles filled the air as adults lifted the children up and down on the ends of sagging pieces of wood. The women on the playground, in typical American fashion, shouted, "Whee… whee," with each elevation and the giggles continued. (My husband later pointed out that since the children speak French or Creole they probably wondered why we kept yelling, "Yes! Yes!")[5]

Unsure of Mitaille's experience with a swing, I sat on one to show her how, and pointed to the swing next to me for her. She sat, once again, right on my lap! What a sight that must have been. I'm barely taller than five feet and Mitaille, at nine or ten years old, was almost the same size.

I pushed off and my feet slipped beneath me. I realized the muddy ground surrounding the swing was not going to

---

[5] Oui, pronounced "whee," is French for "yes."

help me. I would need to stick my feet straight down to get enough support to push both of us. Straight down, however, was covered by six inches of stagnant, muddy (possibly mosquito infested) water. But another breakthrough was imminent, so I plunged my feet down to the bottom of that puddle and pushed the human pendulum into motion. With all my might I pumped my legs. A little higher... a little higher still... and then I saw it. From the side, her cheekbones were lifting. Little lines were forming next to her eyes. I caught a glimpse of light coming from her face. She was smiling! Hours from our initial meeting. Hours spent in relative silence. There it was. And it was beautiful!

She wrapped her legs around mine and began pumping with me. Both our bodies and our spirits were soaring. I was so excited that I began mimicking my seesawing friends with an extended, "Wheeee..." as we went up and forward. I think she may have giggled. Like Pavlov with his dogs, I continued searching for the same response. "Wheeee," I'd say.

Her smile grew. Then I heard it. It was quiet, almost a whisper, but it was there. "Whee," she said.

It had taken all day to get there. It had taken the Holy Spirit to guide me at her pace, not mine. It had taken us to a beautiful place.

The rest of the afternoon was incredible. We smiled. We laughed. We played together. As it turned out, she loved my sunglasses. I wasn't sure I was ever going to get them back!

You may think this was the beginning of a wonderful week spent with Mitaille. Oddly, though, that's not how it unfolded. In fact, my only interactions with her on the upcoming days were a mutual smile in passing. As I think back it's interesting to see how we all have a role in God's plan. My time with Mitaille was for but a day. Seeds were planted. Doors were opened. But the Lord had someone else for her to spend time with that week. And somewhere else for me to be.

The Wheelchair Brigade

As I mentioned earlier, New Life Children's Home is a rescue orphanage. Each of the 150 children came here literally on the verge of dying. With the loving help of the caregivers, called "baby mothers," most of them run and jump and play as if they have al-

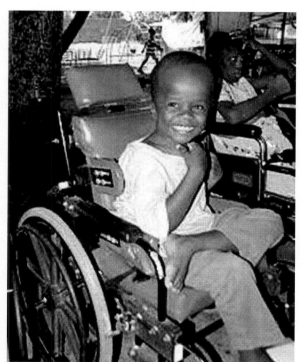

ways been healthy. But there are others whose damage is too extensive. Cribs and wheelchairs, and in one case restraints, hold these children day after day. It was to these children I was drawn.

Protected by the shade of the second mango tree, farthest from the gate, was the wheelchair brigade. Approximately 10 children of various ages and capacities were gathered there. The leader of the gang was Chinaido. His innate sense of humor and infectious smile were an invitation to come and stay awhile. Like any great comic, timing is everything. As Miriam was introducing him to us, he searched the crowd for eye contact. Once he knew he had it, he locked us in his sights, and without breaking eye contact he slowly reached down for his foot. With great flexibility and a growing grin, he put his big toe in his mouth, bit down gently, and giggled as he let go and let his foot dangle from his teeth as the crowd roared with laughter!

Another beautiful girl, Isabella, sat in her wheelchair just to his right. She was much younger than Chinaido, and not able to interact as much. However, her eyes lit up like precious jewels and she'd shoot you a huge smile, almost a giggle, when you called her by name. "Isabella, Isabella, my pretty girl," I would sing. "Isabella, I know your name."

I thought of how important it is to each of us to realize someone knows our name. I was hit by a flood of emotions tied tightly to times when someone did, or didn't, remember my name. In that moment, it struck me as if the Lord himself were whispering in my ear, "Natalie, *I* know her name." "I," I thought. The Lord of all creation knows her name. The Lord of our lives knows her name. The world's most perfect personification of Love, knows her name. While I recognize how important it is for us to connect with these children, it is vital for that connection to always lead them to Jesus. From then on, I sang, "Isabella, Isabella, Jesus knows your name. You are precious to Him and He knows your name." Her attention remained fixed on my words, and I believe He was there, visiting with us, on that special day.

Others in the gang were much more difficult to interact with. All had some type of physical challenge. Some were also developmentally delayed. Each day I'd play with them for a minute or two, lingering with those who responded, though usually it was just a smile, a giggle, or an outstretched arm.

A few of the children, however, seemed to be barely more than a bodily shell. I was careful each day to greet each one, but was at a loss on how to do more than that.

Earlier that morning, Pastor Stan had come to me, tapped me on the shoulder, and told me he had someone he wanted me to meet, Valerie. I fol-lowed with great an-ticipation. When we got up to the build-ing, I was surprised to see Valerie sitting in a chair on the ve-randa. I don't know why, but I had pic-tured her lying in a bed. I also don't know why, but somehow the chair felt a little more chal-lenging to me. The first interaction with Valerie for me was awkward. I had re-hearsed how to ap-proach her, and now something as minute as a change in posture set me back for a minute. I wasn't sure how she would react to my getting close. I wanted to share the warmth of touch, but felt almost afraid. Her eyes were like radar, honing in on me and tracking each step, each move I made. It sent my mind reeling with questions. How could I know what she was thinking? Would she feel threat-ened by my approach? Did I need to be careful of her lashing out? I

took a deep breath, and thought to myself, "I can do all things through Christ who strengthens me."[6]

With the Lord's strength, I began to talk to Valerie, careful to touch her arm or knee as I spoke. The touch of my hand and the sound of my voice brought an expression that said she was confused, with just a hint of upturned lips as if she might be considering responding with a smile. I stayed with her awhile, but eventually returned to my place on the work crew, afraid that I wasn't holding up my end of the work that needed to be done. (In retrospect, I was unaware that I was already doing "the work that needed to be done.") At every chance, though, I returned for brief encounters with Valerie. We were just getting warmed up.

That afternoon I asked (with gestures since I didn't know the language) if I could help feed one of the children. There was a hydrocephalic baby boy that needed his lunch. I held him in my arms and did my best to spoon-feed him. I never did find out how old he was, but he was small enough, and weak enough, that he couldn't hold his own head up. With his unusually large head and desperately small body he seemed more fragile than the rest.

While I sat on the bench feeding him, my back ached beyond belief from the heavy lifting we had done all morning. I changed positions over and over to try to find a way to hold him and minimize the pain. Stan walked by while I was feeding him. I felt guilty. I wondered if he would be upset that I wasn't working with the others. But something drew me there. He smiled, so I stayed.

Shortly after I began, one of the caregivers settled next to me to feed another baby, a delicate, tiny girl. She was sitting in an infant seat. Her legs were dangling over the bottom edge, seeming a bit too long for the rest of her. She wore a pink polka-dot dress, just

---

[6] Philippians 4:13

like the ones I had always envisioned buying if I had a daughter of my own. She had very little hair but had a braid on top of her head, and a couple more in the back. Her skin was milk chocolate and perfect. She had just enough energy to tilt her head back and lift her eyes in my direction. I glanced over at her and smiled. Much to my surprise her eyes lit up, and she responded in kind with a huge, heart-grabbing grin. As I continued feeding the first child, my attention kept turning back to the baby in the infant seat near my feet. Her big brown eyes held my gaze. When she smiled, which was often, you could see tiny little teeth, gleaming white with little spots of greenish stains. When she moved the muscles in her lips to smile, her eyes sparkled. It was infectious, forcing anyone who caught a glimpse to smile back.

But that's not what was holding my attention captive. With each breath she took came a terrible rattle in her throat and chest that everyone could hear. With just enough nurse's training to be dangerous, I began amateur diagnostics to determine the problem. Bronchitis, maybe. Croup? No cough. I talked to Stan later, and he even suggested tuberculosis, a disease we rarely ever have 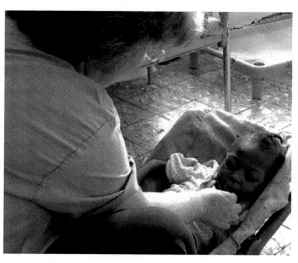 to think about in our country. I knew I had to find out.

I knew that on Wednesday, when we returned, I also had another child to visit. A child named Marilee.

Evening, October 4

Today we began work in Haiti at New Life Children's Home. The first part of the day was very physical and extremely hot. Between the heat and my lack of conditioning, I found it very difficult. I kept up for the most part, but did need to take an extra break or two to get out of the sun for a while. Together we unloaded the vast majority of a 40-foot tractor trailer full of food, clothing, desks, and medical supplies. We stopped only when the container began sinking into the muddy ground beneath it and tipped dangerously to one side.

To be honest, I am still processing the whole experience. It's interesting because I feel the same way right now as I did after the first day of work in Mississippi. Dare I say a little disappointed? We worked hard, but I did not come away with a sense of accomplishing what God called me here for. Maybe I just need a day to adjust and find my way.

After dinner Stan lead us in a devotion time designed to help us process our day. It was very powerful for me. There were things I saw and heard that day that made such an impression on me. But then came our first exposure to the artist in Jim as he shared his first slide show with us. To my surprise it was set to the song, "Follow You." I sobbed as I took in images of our team and the children and heard the words that I had prayed so often. I thank the Lord for confirmation that He had heard my prayers.

I am alone in my room right now. I thought people were heading back to the rooms but I guess I was wrong. That's OK. As much as I value the time spent together, I feel it's very important for me to take time to think and pray and ask for God's leading day by day.

I'd like to write more but I'm so tired and still processing.

I pray, Lord, you will use me mightily tomorrow. Show me why I'm here. Let me love someone for you tomorrow. Amen.

Meet Me at the Light Pole

Morning, Tuesday, October 5

Rain. Mud. For the first few days Haiti fooled me into believing the day was hot and sunny and the rain came only in early evening, and was somehow a welcomed nuisance that brought with it slightly cooler weather. This routine, so I thought, allowed Haitians to do what they needed to do during the daylight hours, and be cooled off in time to sleep. But this morning I learned the rain can sneak in at any time and bring with it gobs and gobs of mud. It has brought cooler temperatures and the dust that has been floating in my eyes each day has settled for a moment. I will therefore look at the rain and call it my friend.

Children play below me just on the other side of the 15-foot wall that protects us from their world. On our side of the wall it is clean, not fancy, but clean. There are a couple of trees growing up through the concrete, and lights to guide us to our rooms at night. On the other side, where the children play, there is a pile several feet high of slimy, pungent garbage growing alongside the wall. From time to time hogs and other animals are heard rummaging through the slop for something to eat. About half way up this wall that forms our fortress are decorative holes designed to lessen the prison-like feel of a wall so high. The holes are too small for anyone to get through, yet they provide the one area of that wall that can be breached, visually, allowing the children a glimpse into our world, and us into theirs. Daily the children make their way up the slippery pile, seemingly unaware of the stench, to peek through into our world, or reach their hands in to the other side. A touch, a hand-out, whatever they can get will do for now. I should be saddened as they call out to me, "My friend, my friend, give me some food. I am hungry." But instead I am angry. Angry at a world that would teach such young boys to be so proficient in their begging.

I am still waiting to fall in love with this place. "Haiti, Oh My Haiti" I heard someone sing on a post-earthquake telethon. But I do not feel it. Is there something wrong with me? Others cannot get over their "ooing and ah-hing" with each mention of the children outside the gate. I admit I did think it was beautiful when we arrived and one of the boys called out "Ann" and "Lauren" (a mother and daughter on our team). They were here a few months ago and they've connected. And their connection gives back with just enough English to let them feel their impact.

I guess that's the difference. My one "connection" was with a girl seemingly mute. And it was beautiful. But she will never call out my name. The children I am trying to reach may never utter a word. But I *will* try to reach them. Lord, I selfishly ask that you somehow show me I've connected. I so desperately want to tell them that you love them. How do I do that?

Evening, October 5

Wow! Thank you, Lord for answered prayer. It has been quite an incredible day. I could write for a very long time just about today. With the children it was the best day yet. With the ride through the city it was the worst. We had a very dangerous incident on our way home. And it's not over yet. I am a bit afraid for our ride in and out of the orphanage tomorrow. On our way out today our bus hit a light pole. Should I say, brushed it. A man wearing what looked like a police uniform ran after the bus yelling and screaming and pounding the side of the bus until we stopped. The bus driver opened the doors of the bus at which point the officer began yelling something at him in Creole. The bus driver decided to yell back. Each man successively raised his voice another decibel in an attempt to overpower the other. During this commotion, the bus driver's son poked his head out the back door to see what was going on. His face was met with the brutal force of another man's fist. He jumped down out of the bus and slammed the back door behind him. The uniformed man moved a step toward the bus as if he was going to board it. The bus driver's assistant quickly ordered him, "Take it outside!" As soon as they were outside, Jevon, our leader, began quietly but forcefully disseminating orders to the men on our team. "Chris, get the front door. Garth, cover the back. Guy, sit in the middle of the women so they are not alone..." (I later learned that Jevon had told Chris that if necessary he would run out the back door and down the street, as if to escape, in order to draw the crowd away from the bus. He asked Chris to take over leadership and get the bus out of there, no matter what happened to him.)

Outside the bus chaos ensued. Men from the community were gathering, some out of curiosity, staring in the windows of the big white bus to see who the strangers were, some joining in on the shouting match, heightening the frenzy that now surrounded us.

Inside the bus, calm preparations began. I quietly re-moved my passport from my backpack and slipped into the inside pocket of my shirt. I then took half of the money I had and stashed it into my bra, leaving the rest of it to satisfy the crowd should they demand our bags.

Outside, men were now shoulder to shoulder across the road, blocking our passage. The shouting continued. The driver of a large oil truck, much too big for the nar-row confines of this dirt road, was trying to get to his ap-pointed destination. As if it would somehow help, he be-gan yelling and screaming for us to move the bus and get out of his way. The other men returned his anger for theirs. They grew more forceful in their demanding, as we later found out, that we pay them $200 for the dam-age to the light pole. The policeman outside joined them, escalating his voice to the point of screaming, as he pounded his fist against the outside of the bus.

In case the chaos had not reached a disturbing enough level, a small pick-up tried to squeeze past the whole scene and ended up stuck in a big hole. From my vantage point, I could almost reach out my window and touch it as men rocked it back and forth in an attempt to get it out of the mud, sloshing filthy water over anyone and anything that dared get too close.

Still the men argued. I suggested we pray. On the outside the chaos continued. On the inside we alternated between quiet prayer, allowing peace to overtake fear, and peeking outside, straining to see if we could overhear anything (as if we could understand Creole!) I'm not sure how long this continued, but with the afternoon sun pounding through my window, it felt like forever.

Jevon used his cell phone to call Pastor Noel and Stan, who were in the pickup truck down the road, to let them know we had a problem. Wisely, Pastor Noel told him to inform the crowd that our leader was in the truck down the road and the negotiation would take place there. One of our Haitian friends, Evens, jumped off the bus and like a brave soldier marched into the middle of the crowd to deliver the message. Like magic, the mayhem moved from the bus to the other end of the street. Only a few curious onlookers remained.

Eventually, our bus drivers got back on the bus, calmly said, "It is just a negotiation," and we were off. I grew up in an Italian family with plenty of loud, macho men. Even so, that was one heck of a negotiation!

All joking aside, I am still very concerned about tomorrow. My understanding of the result of the negotiation is that the driver promised to bring $50 tomorrow to pay for the damage. We are a big white bus full of white people in the middle of Port-Au-Prince, Haiti – a little hard to sneak by! And we are traveling on a road barely wide enough for us, full of holes and water, with no escape route. I am praying for safety and guidance and wisdom for our leaders.

But back to the children and the orphanage. When we first got there today I headed for the orphanage building to finish some painting. I never made it through the door! A little boy ran up to hug me, then a little girl, then another. I leaned down to greet them and the force of their hugs knocked me off my feet–literally! Once I regained enough balance to sit up, they climbed up on my lap. I could have used an extra knee but managed to keep them all happy taking turns from sitting on one knee or the other, or standing behind me playing with, or should I say inspecting, my straight, lighter hair. They were fascinated by my hair, my glasses, my face, anything they could touch. Thus began a day of no work projects and all chil-

dren: swings, bottles, diapers, walks holding hands and little ones grabbing my arms and wrapping them tightly
around their little bodies as they held on for dear life. I
don't have enough ink or paper to recount all the moments. The hunger there, for love as well as food, is so
great that the flow of children is constant. But there are a
few that will live on in my heart and mind forever. I have
introduced two of them to you already. They are The
Girls on the Veranda.

The Girls on the Veranda

Each day as I entered the orphanage property, I glanced toward the building where the small children and girls sleep to see
the girls on the veranda. There were often young children in cribs
or infant seats sitting there with the women of the house. The
younger ones changed from day to day, but there were three girls
who were there permanently.

In the right-hand corner of the veranda was a crib. Not a tiny portable crib like those that line the halls inside. This was a full-
sized crib, with a full-sized child inside. Maniella made her home
there day after day. She was bigger than most of the children in
cribs, by a lot. Since I cannot speak Creole, I never did learn her di-
agnosis, but I suspect it might be cerebral palsy. If you called out
her name and gave her a smile, her glowing face acknowledged
your outreach.

With her swallowing reflex stunted, her mouth is nearly always open and full of moist saliva, tempting gnats and flies to keep
her company. I tried to swat them away but my efforts were futile.
She laughed at my attempts, and made sounds as if she was trying
to talk to me, though none of those sounds were intelligible.

For the past three days I have taken time to talk and
sing to her and call her by name. I touch and hold her

hand and draw it to me to gently kiss it. I have learned to remove my glasses first, though, or she'll move with the quickness of a jackrabbit and grab them right off my face!

Just to the side of Maniella is Valerie, the girl Stan had introduced me to earlier. She is considerably more than developmentally challenged. Something insidious has robbed her of her mind in such a way that she must be restrained day and night. With her wrists and ankles tied she sits in a chair, about three feet from Maniella, and rocks and groans and stares. I can't even begin to fathom what is happening behind those big, brown eyes. What I do know is that if you release her from her restraints she will bang her head against the wall and chew on her clothing. So how do you offer human touch to a girl whose hands are tied to a wrought iron chair?

The third girl, Marilee, has grabbed my heart and compels me to seek her out each day. The first day was just a smile from her infant seat as I held and fed a little boy next to her. I could not get over that smile, and it was almost as if she knew it. She would look up at me through the corner of her eyes tempting me to stay. It worked. While I was there to minister to Maniella and Valerie, I just had to find that smile again. I held her for quite some time today. Feeding her is very difficult because she doesn't swallow easily and her raspy, labored breathing intimidates me as I try to be careful not to let her choke. Her arms and legs are so skinny I feel as if she could break. In fact, I took my thumb and pinkie and wrapped them around her leg just above the ankle, with room to spare. I wasn't sure of her age but did notice she was wearing a one-piece that was sized 18 months. Why is she so tiny? How old is she?

It would take me a couple of days to learn the answers.

Maniella

As I stepped up onto the veranda on the third day, I realized I had found my place, my purpose for the week. The sun was shining brightly and two of the baby mothers greeted me as if welcoming a friend. They had taken refuge in the shade of the veranda, along with several of the smaller children, and my three girls, of course.

As I maneuvered the obstacle course of cribs and infant seats, I stopped briefly to pick up Marilee. Jim was standing by the crib where Maniella lives. As I gave a warm "good morning" to Marilee, Jim exclaimed, "Oh, Maniella, you know that voice, don't you?" To my surprise, and delight, Maniella was trying to turn in the direction of my voice. I propped Marilee on my hip and scooted

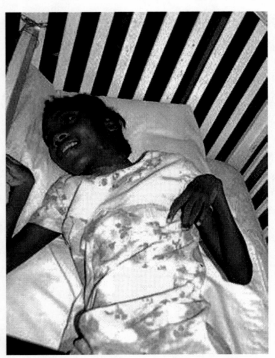

over to Maniella. Excitedly she reached out her hand for a good-morning kiss. She may not have been able to call out my name, but her recognition, and our connection, was unmistakable.

Maniella, like all the other children, was well taken care of. Each day she was washed, sprinkled with some nice cool powder and dressed in clean clothes. She was a beautiful young lady, but was being held hostage by her retracted, weakened muscles. I couldn't help but wonder how her life would be changed with something as simple as physical therapy. Daily exercising of those arms and legs would, I thought, make such a difference in her range of motion. I also can't help but wonder if she had been born in the US, would she have had the opportunity for an education. Her eyes told me there is so much more to her than we could see.

Beside her bed that day was a wheelchair. It was about her size and I wondered if she would be released from the bars of the crib to sit up for awhile. Half in halted English, half in sign language, one of the baby mothers and I talked about the possibility. Unfortunately, she explained that because of her limited range of motion, she was too stiff for the chair. They had tried, but she just screamed to be back in bed.

I thought of a friend of mine from high school who had CP. He was very bright, did very well in school, and became an author as an adult. With the help of his electric wheelchair he not only attended school, but also football games, basketball games, and even the prom. I remember him on the dance floor, using the controls to move side to side, and even a few disco-like spins!

At 17, Maniella is about the age now that he was when he was in my memory. The same age, but worlds apart. I cried inside for the loss of what could have been. And I wondered, "Does she ever dance in her own dreams?"

Valerie

As the days passed, so did my fear of the wrought iron chair. Instead I looked forward to my time with Valerie each day. I not only talked to her, but also I showered her with hugs and gentle touches. "Jesus loves you, Valerie," I said as I touched her face, or hair, or arms. I prayed that the combination of human touch and the Holy Spirit's love would heal some part of her, somehow reaching the girl behind the big brown eyes.

On Thursday I decided to bring a book with me. My intention was to just sit and quietly read to Valerie. The book was a sort of devotional for women. I thought the encouraging words, even in

a language she was unaccustomed to, might bring a sense of peace to her corner of the veranda. As I prepared to read, I sat down on the cement next to her chair. She looked at me curiously as I was now much shorter than her and somewhat vulnerable, a position I never would have taken just a few days earlier.

I began to read. As I did, I made sure to look up and into her eyes which were now completely fixed on me. I'd glance down for another few words and reach out to her arm, engage her eyes, and recite the words I'd just taken in. I felt so awkward, but stumbled through until something stopped me. The Spirit moved my attention to the one thing I had virtually ignored all week. Her hand. Her wrought iron chair bound hand, with its palm facing up and empty. It reminded me of times I've cried out to God, arms down, hands outstretched, and palms empty, waiting for the Lord to fill the void. Only *her* wrists were bound to a chair. What is it that binds me? Unlike the children who had greeted us earlier with hugs and handshakes, I had no doubt that *her* hand had rarely been touched. It beckoned me, called me to draw near and fill the void.

Slowly, carefully, I wrapped my hand around hers. She stared intently at our hands. Her fingers still pointed downward, her palm now engulfed in my grasp like a one-sided handshake. Still I read. I told her I loved her. I told her Jesus loved her. She stared. I read some more.

Then it happened. In answer to a prayer whispered in my journal three days earlier, it happened. With her eyes fixed on our hands, with the intensity of one who had been paralyzed for years and had to focus and will her muscles to move, she curled her fingers upward and held my hand.

Tears filled my eyes as my lips formed a quivering smile. Her eyes asked mine if what she had just done was okay. She needed to know I approved of her touch, her grasp, her reaching back. My eyes said, "Yes."

I laid down the book and abandoned my reading for a much more powerful story. As we each glanced back and forth from making eye contact to marveling at our now mutually embraced hands, I sensed we were sharing in a similar sort of disbelief. For I could swear I heard us both say, "I can't believe she's holding my hand."

Marilee

All week I had been growing closer and closer to the three girls on the veranda. Marilee, in particular, had stolen my heart. At lunch on our second day at the orphanage I asked Miriam to tell me about her. She explained that Marilee was one of the more recently rescued children. She had come from another orphanage that had tried, but couldn't help her. The breathing difficulty is due to a problem with her trachea. Miriam explained that she needs to go to the US for a very delicate surgical procedure. She also said that Marilee's condition is very serious and that if she got sick at all, even a cold or the flu, she could die. My heart breaks for children who so desperately need what my own children have so readily accessible.

Before we went back out for our afternoon work, I asked Miriam one last question. It was a simple question: "How old is she?" The answer stole my breath, choking me and forcing tears from my eyes to relieve the pressure building in my mind. This beautiful baby in the 18-month-sized, pink polka-dot dress was somewhere between four and five years old.

I spent a good part of the rest of the week with Marilee in my arms. We grew very attached to each other. On Thursday she seemed a bit listless. I touched her forehead with my lips, a mom's makeshift thermometer, and realized she had quite a fever. I told one of the baby mothers. At first, she touched Marilee's forehead, smiled, and said, "No, no, no la fev. No la fev." But my lips don't lie and I kept insisting "la fev, la fev" and shaking my head yes as if that would make me more convincing. Finally, she took me to Nurse Mimi whose digital thermometer confirmed the fever, 101 degrees. Miriam's words swirled in my head: "If she gets sick at all, even a cold or the flu, she could die."

We had been called to board the bus to return to the hotel for the evening, but I just couldn't go without addressing this. I ran to Miriam's office and found her meeting with the doctor who takes care of the children at the orphanage (God's timing is always perfect). I told her about Marilee's listlessness and fever. She and the doctor went to see her immediately. I had to leave. I didn't want to. I had only known her for a few days, yet I felt like a mother leaving her sick child. I followed them down the stairs and reluctantly turned right while they went left. I boarded the bus with a heavy heart. I prayed for her all evening.

The next day we faced yet another day of Haitian heat. Upon arriving at the orphanage, I rushed to find Marilee. She seemed a little better. Still, with a slight fever, the heat made it quite uncomfortable to hold her all day. But she and I both wanted more than anything to stay close. In an attempt to find a comfortable position, I discovered something very exciting! I sat down on the ground and held her so she straddled my leg. I took her skinny little feet and gently rubbed them on the ground so she could feel it. Suddenly those tiny little white teeth were shining at me as she stood straight up! She couldn't balance without my help, but proud as could be she showed me that even though they were barely visible over her bones, she could use those leg muscles to stand!

"Look at you!" I repeated over and over. "What a big girl you are! So big!" Until then I had assumed she could not support her own weight. Between the fact that she was always in a crib or infant seat, and her overall weakened state due to the fever, I didn't even think to try. But *she* did! I caught a momentary glimpse of the little girl she could one day be, running like the rest of the rescued, healed children at New Life Children's Home. What a glorious day that will be!

Shortly after my time reading to Valerie, I took Marilee out to a bench to sit quietly in the shade of the mango tree. By some miracle, we were the only two there, and I longed for the time to just pray and process. So much had happened over such a short time.

As we sat on the bench together, one of the older boys came over to give me the book I had left on the ground near Valerie. Not knowing my name he said, "Excuse me, Baby Mother." I smiled with pride, and now remember with tears, that he would think to call me that. How I wished it were true.

I Could Have Missed the Blessings

Friday, October 8, 2010

It has been a noisy morning! We were awakened to a hog violently objecting to the evening's pork-filled menu. Goats have been bleating, roosters crowing, voices by the wall, voices in the distance...

After about an hour of chaos, I stepped out onto the balcony to spend some time with the Lord. I was shocked at the amount of sludge rushing down the street like a river. Tributaries fed it from every direction, washing past the hundreds of tents below. Just yesterday I was thankful for the rain as I hoped it would bring relief from the heat. I never considered the fact that the same rain that brought my relief would bring disease infested waters flooding through the beds of so many below. Forgive me, Lord, for selfish thinking.

Today's scripture is Acts 7:54–60, "The Stoning of Stephen." Not sure I like that since we are about to take a drive I am not convinced is safe. But I will trust the Lord (and pray more fervently than ever for safe travel). It just dawned on me that I do that out of habit every day. Today, it seems a little different.

On Friday I tried to spend a little more time with the children in the wheelchair brigade. I still spent most of the day with my three girls on the veranda, but something kept bothering me and calling my attention to the children under the mango tree. I must confess: what was actually bothering me was one young woman in particular. I had noticed her every day, but had done nothing. For-give me, but I had largely ignored her.

With the body of a full-grown woman, she sat completely still and silent. In fact, the only movement I ever saw was when one of the caregivers would come to her and scoot her back up in her chair. Her limbs were contracted and her neck permanently tilted back leaving her face pointing toward the sky. To this day, I'm not sure why I felt so intimidated by her, but I did.

Now Friday was here. I only had one more day and I could not get her out of my mind. With no particular plan, I approached her. It must have been quite comical to watch from a distance. Be-ing as short as I am, coupled with her posture positioning her face upward, I had to lean on the arm of her chair and stand on my toes and stretch as far as I could to make sure she could see me.

For the first time all week she moved. Not her entire body– just her eyes. She moved her eyes and looked right at me. "Well, hello there beautiful," I responded. Suddenly a smile crossed her face. My heart sank as the realization hit me and I heard myself think, "Oh dear God, someone's in there!"

I wanted to celebrate and cry in shame at the same time. I gently put my hand on her cheek and, much like with Valerie, told her how much Jesus loves her. She smiled wider and made a noise in response. (Forgive me, Lord, for not reaching out sooner.)

I took several opportunities throughout the day and a half I had left to spend time with her. She may not have understood what I was saying. But she understood the Spirit with which it was said. I only wish I hadn't taken so long to get past my fears. But eventual-ly, with the help of the Holy Spirit, I did. Thankfully. Otherwise, we both would have missed the blessing.

Evening, October 8

We made it! It was not uneventful (not sure it ever is) but it was not frightening like yesterday. We drove to the orphanage a different way so we wouldn't have to pass by the spot where the light pole was. After carefully navigating the bus through a turn meant for a VW Beetle, we breathed a collective sigh of relief thinking we were home free. All we had to do was pass a tent city in a field, take another hairpin turn or two, and we'd be there. It would have worked, too, if not for the two feet of mud the driver tried to plow through—and failed.

The sight of this big, white stuck-in-the-mud bus was quite an attraction. Men, women, and children came out of their tents to see what the commotion was all about. The adults, for the most part, watched from a distance as our leaders walked around the bus and analyzed our predicament. The children, however, jumped into action. As I looked out my window I saw tiny children with tiny hands collecting stones, probably three or four per handful, and placing them behind the wheels of the bus! In this tense moment, we were so blessed by their acts of kindness. They were so proud of their efforts. I'm not even sure where they were getting the stones, but they kept coming. Unfortunately it would take about a week for those tiny hands to be able to collect enough stones to make any difference at all. It was obvious, we had to get off the bus and walk the rest of the way.

As we began our walk to the orphanage, we heard a man call out over a loud speaker, announcing our plight. I have to admit, although I was thankful, I also wished he'd wait until we were safely back inside the orphanage walls before telling the whole neighborhood we were stranded. The call to action was answered by 30 men. They worked for three hours with their bare hands to dig our bus out of the mud. The image of the angry men from yesterday seemed to temporarily melt away knowing these Haitians were working so hard to help us. Granted we did pay them. In all the 30 men worked for three hours to split $20. The hard work of the men, the generous outpouring from the children, and the smiles from the women of the camp transformed my view of the people in the tent city.

As we headed out for the orphanage, we walked behind the lead vehicle, not sure of how far we had to walk. We moved past the tent city, down the dirt road, around the corner and past the armed guard at the orphanage gate. Somehow this twenty-something in jeans and a T-shirt carrying an automatic weapon suddenly looked like a friend! My view of him had been transformed.

This day has truly been a blessing! Thank you, Lord, for using mud to help us grow.

Transformation

Transformation. God's transformative powers are astounding! Whenever people reach out to share His love, His love transforms.

Certainly, on a short-term missions trip there is the transforming of the physical world. Walls get painted, screen doors get fixed, floors get tiled, and 40-foot containers full of food and supplies get emptied to allow the contents to be put to their intended use.

There is, however, another kind of transformation. It takes place as God reaches in and uses that time away from home to mold and fashion you into the man or woman you were created to be. Often you feel it; you sense His work within. Sometimes it becomes so evident that others catch a glimpse or hint of it. But every so often the change becomes absolutely undeniable.

One such transformation took place in the heart and life of one of my travel partners, Guy.

On the afternoon our trip began, Guy arrived at the church with his wife, Maria. I thought it sweet that he hardly let go of her embrace the entire time we stood there waiting for the last few stragglers to arrive. I was unaware at that time that he was holding on to her for support as he was actually considering backing out of the trip. Fear and anxiety taunted him that day, and had been doing so for quite some time. When it was time to leave, however, Guy was in the van with the rest of the team.

The next morning, as we sat in the Fort Lauderdale airport waiting for one last flight to take us to Haiti, I sensed something was wrong. Sweat on his brow, panic-stricken eyes, slightly shaking hands; anxiety had gripped him and was shaking him like an angry foe. (In retrospect we can confirm there was an angry foe, for God had a plan to work good through Guy that week!)

Guy confirmed his anxiety, and I placed my hand firmly on his arm and prayed for God's peace. And I kept praying, throughout that day and the next week. And so began the transformation.

Here's an excerpt from his journal:

> Arrived at Port-au-Prince, Haiti 10-4-10. Stepped away from my flight and onto the glass deck. Local music group playing down below made arriving festive, even though the melody was repetitive. My attention was drawn out the window at the horizon, struck by the awesome beauty of the distant mountain range and perfect sky. My feelings were already raw with anticipation. I wept! God is working in me!

One of the few things I knew about Guy before our trip is that he is a toy designer, trucks in particular. He loves to draw. It is one of his God-given talents. I tell you this because as we each think about our gifts and talents, we can sometimes wonder if they can be used on the mission field. We can always see how someone else's can be, but wonder if ours will fall short. But what if I told you that God took Guy's ability to draw trucks, and used it in a mighty way?

His journal continues:

I returned to the New Life Children's Home with high expectations; hopes of better connecting with the Haitian workers. Today, I drew Miriam's Toyota Land Cruiser; a 2010 model only sold in second and third-world countries. Little did I know that sharing the drawing with Lans, the head of Maintenance, would open doors. Together we worked on building a new three-door kitchen cabinet from scratch. Throughout the build, Lans would consistently take my pen to write. I would draw a picture of what we needed to do, and he would translate. It was awesome. Other men came by to listen and see what we were doing and wanted to experience this funny American!

The working conditions were primitive and not what I'd consider safe. Dragging a heavy table saw out from under a shelter, through water, to cut plywood on a muddy concrete sidewalk, these were not the working conditions I was used to! I quickly learned to just relax, wait, be patient, because the task would get done, but on Haiti time. By the time the day was done, Lans said I was his "Bon Ami." His "friend."

That night at the hotel, Guy found himself alone in his room. He was so pleased with the day, and all they had accomplished, but the anxiety and emotions were flooding back in. He was alone in a foreign place, unaccustomed to the environment, the food, the constant smell of diesel and smoke, the language, and unsure of where to turn for help if he needed it.

As he sat struggling in silence, he realized that it wasn't just about Haiti. He was dealing simultaneously with these present feelings as well as unresolved memories. Familiar feelings flooded in. Feelings of being dropped into a setting where he felt alone and unsure. He had felt this struggle before, a long time ago, a long way from here. It was difficult, but he had to work through it. God was transforming a very deep part of him so that he could be used as an instrument to transform others. It was not an easy night, and he never saw it coming. But understanding the paralyzing past allowed him to begin to move toward his future. Healed. Transformed. As each day passed, Guy was growing right before our eyes.

Due to the highly energized ordeal of hitting the pole yesterday, a different route to the orphanage was chosen this morning. Note: Our big white bus stands out! We ended up taking a road that was more like an alley. The driver did his best to make a 90-degree turn, with literally a hand's thickness of space between the bus and wall. The entire bus cheered as we cleared the turn and moved on.

Eventually, we came to the end of that alley to a field filled with tents. The road split at the entrance, with a dry road to the right and a deep, muddy, rutted path straight ahead. The lead car turned right onto the dry path. We paused for a moment and to all of our surprise the driver gunned the engine, plowing straight into the mud!! A-duh! In moments we were stuck in two feet of mud. It was obvious we weren't going to be able to just push the bus out, so while the drivers stayed to figure out what to do, we grabbed our gear and walked!

After walking three fourths of a mile, we approached the steel orphanage gate. It slid to one side, with the help of the armed guard, to welcome us into this tranquil compound. Stepping through the threshold of the gate, I felt a sense of triumph. We had made it! Not only from the hike through unknown territory, but survived overcoming fears of being in such unfamiliar surroundings, living conditions, and all that is Haiti!

What his journal doesn't tell you is that during that hike to the orphanage, Guy got beyond his anxiety and took very seriously his responsibility to me and our other travel partner, Pat. I can still hear him calling out my name and instructing me to stay to his right while we walked, positioning himself between me and the tents we were passing. He moved past his fears in order to protect us. Growth. Transformation.

Later that day my work partner became extremely ill with fever. With him out of commission, I had to finish repairs on one last screen.

The kids were rollerblading and running all over. I needed to find a quiet place, out of the sun, away from the noise for I was beat, dirty, and it was 95 degrees with 90% humidity. In the middle of the compound was an oasis! A small, concrete patio island, with a shade tree growing in the middle.

I got to work but before too long someone came to see what I was doing. At first, all I saw was shoes near the edge of the screen. Those shoes belonged to Ones (pronounced O-nes), one of the older orphans. He had a deformed right arm, and dragged his right leg. He watched, then immediately began to help. He was great. I spoke English and bad Creole, but he totally got me! After awhile, I gave him the tool I was using to press the screen webbing into the frame. He did a perfect job, too!

We finished, cut off the excess screen, and walked to where the repaired screens were being stored. We took a few steps, and then I said he should carry the screen because he did it! Ones beamed and was so proud, for he was useful! That day, Ones changed my life in so many ways. Basically, Ones was ministering to me.

After dropping off the screens we walked to the main house porch to rest and have a snack and to wait for the bus back to the hotel. What happened next was so amazing! I took out my drawing pad to show Ones my drawings, one of which was of the Toyota Land Cruiser that belonged to the orphanage. Ones was so impressed. I drew a monster truck for him! I even put his name on the door.

The bus arrived at 4:00 and it was time to go. Ones was beaming and I was so pleased and grateful. Pleased to bring so much happiness to someone who has nothing but the bare essentials, and grateful for the opportunity to share my talent with someone who really appreciates it!

God was working here!

Guy had found his voice – it came in the form of a pencil and a sketch pad.

Friday evening as the team sat around sharing our experiences of the day, Guy mentioned to me he had spent very little time with the younger children. Since I had spent so much time around the more challenged children, I told him he should do the same, as the next morning was our last day at the orphanage. I encouraged him to put down the tools and pick up a child. I was wrong, at least in the way I envisioned it. Yes, it was good for Guy to experience, even briefly, the smaller or more challenged children. For me, that is where I belonged. But each of us has a different role to play in God's design. Mine is not yours, and yours is not mine. I had found my place, but so had Guy. I just didn't realize it. As the Scripture says:

> The body is a unit, though it is made up of many parts; and though all its parts are many, they form one body. So it is with Christ. For we were all baptized by one Spirit into one body—whether Jews or Greeks, slave or free—and we were all given the one Spirit to drink.
>
> Now the body is not made up of one part but of many. If the foot should say, "Because I am not a hand I do not belong to the body," it would not for that reason cease to be part of the body. And if the ear should say, "Because I am not an eye, I do not belong to the body," it would not for that reason cease to be part of the body. If the whole body were an eye, where would the sense of hearing be? If the whole body were an ear, where would the sense of smell be? But in fact God has arranged the parts in the body, every one of them, *just as he wanted them to be*. If they were all one part, where would the body be? As it is, there are many parts but one body.
>
> I Corinthians 12:12-20 NIV

As Guy so simply, but beautifully, wrote that day:

> Last full day. Half day at the orphanage. This day, for a change, during a nice break in my work routine, I headed to spend time with the children. While at the children's home, I was introduced to a 17-year-old girl that was confined to a crib! She responded to her name. I took her small hand and held it for the longest time, all the while calling her name and talking to her. These kids

responded to touch but very few engage them or even see them!

I later played with a young boy confined to a wheelchair who could barely walk without assistance. I picked him up by his arms, allowing his body to hang and feet to touch the ground. He laughed as his feet touched each step descending from the porch. I put him on the swings and gently rocked him for the longest while. Such a simple thing brought great joy and laughter and I think made his day! I then held him for awhile. He was tiring so I placed him back in his wheelchair. He gazed at me, smiling, then promptly scooted away.

As I stood there, gazing around, taking it all in, I heard my name. Ones had found me and we greeted each other. He wanted to walk. Taking his left hand, he gripped my right forearm and began walking. In Haiti this is a sign of respect between a younger man and an elder. The amazing thing for me is that in less than 24 hours I had bonded with this young man. He touched my soul.

We walked together stopping at the playground for a few moments, then proceeded over the grass to the gravel road. We talked and walked the gravel road. As we came around the bend, I paused for a moment and I exclaimed, "Wait a minute! Are you taking me to the container, so I can help unload it?"

"Yes!" he replied, smiling.

I sternly looked at him, then laughed and said, "Fine! Let's go!" I then took his arm in my hand and we walked together to the container. He was so happy, beaming and filled with joy! I thought to myself this might have been the very first time that an older man showed him kindness and compassion. It was great.

> Moments later I was part of a human chain unloading
> 2,000 pounds of beans to stack and store in a warehouse.

As we all worked that line to unload our last container of the trip, Guy was beaming. Suddenly, he turned toward me and another woman with a look in his eyes, as if he'd been struck by lightning. He gasped briefly, as if something had taken his breath away, the way an infant does when a breeze hits his face. It must have been the breath of God breathing new life into him, for his next words amazed us. He jokingly said, " You know, now I am a Missionary man, and I know the words to that song!"

I had no idea what he was talking about.

"I can sing that song! I can sing those words to Missionary Man!" He insisted. He was referring to a song by the Eurythmics about a man who was strong and powerful and went into the jungles and hard to reach places to tell people about the Bible and the love of God.

We asked him to tell us how it goes. He put his hands on his hips, puffed out his chest Superman style, and belted it out!

> Don't mess with a missionary man
>
> Oh the missionary man, he's got God on his side
>
> He's got the saints and apostles backin' up from behind
>
> Black eyed looks from those bible books...

We laughed hysterically as he didn't even hesitate when he reached a part of the song he couldn't remember. He confidently sang, "Blah, blah, blah..." He was too energized to care!

He sang that song for us in the warehouse. Then again on the bus. And again that night at dinner… and even in the aisle of the plane as we landed back in Boston the next night!

His last journal entry read:

> Saying good-bye was hard. Harder still to say good-bye to Ones. Before leaving I made a commitment to sponsor him and remain part of his life.

Maria, Guy's wife, honored his commitment to Ones. Together they continue to support him and be a part of his life through letters and, of course, pictures. Ones now has a skill (screen repair) *and* a family that cares for him. Another life transformed.

Guy undertook quite a journey! One week earlier he held his wife in a deep embrace, drawing from her strength and support. On the day we returned, he couldn't wait to do the same. Only this time, she would sense a strength from him instead. Despite anxiety and fear, he stepped onto a plane in obedience. One week later he stepped off a plane a "Missionary Man." God's transformative powers. Astounding.

The Invisible Man

Saturday, October 9

> Today was incredible. Powerful. Not necessarily in a positive way—but eye opening and heart breaking.
>
> It began with our last day at the orphanage. Another 40-foot trailer was delivered yesterday full of food and other supplies. We began our day by unloading that (though I did very little because there were so many of us working on that one task).

I spent my last couple of hours with Marilee. She had a fever again and is now on an antibiotic. It breaks my heart to hear her gasp for each breath.

It was so very hot today that once again I struggled to find a way to hold her that would be comfortable for her. But the shade of the trees and the slight breeze helped me out. I also discovered yesterday that she likes the swing. Not a big, excited, pump-with-all-your-heart swing. Just a lay-back-on-my-lap-and-feel-the-gentle-movement-and-slight-breeze-cool-your-face swing.

She seemed a bit weaker today. Still in good spirits, she generously doled out smiles and even blessed me with giggles that somehow made me laugh and cry at the same time.

I think I kissed her about a thousand times today. We have become so attached to each other over these few days. It both thrills me and breaks my heart for I know that soon there will be no more visits for this "Baby Mother."

I wonder if she'll miss me. In a strange, selfish way, I hope so. But then again, for her sake, I pray not.

After saying our last good-byes to the children, we loaded the bus to begin our tour of Port-au-Prince. It was the first tourism type thing we'd done all week. I was interested in seeing some of the downtown areas, like the Presidential Palace. Those who had been here a few months before were anxious to see if any progress had been made. Oddly, they did seem to recognize some things as being better. Having not experienced the before pictures, it was difficult for me to imagine what I was seeing as progress.

For what seemed like hours we sat in the hot bus fighting traffic and noise and rain in an attempt to get to a

market. I secretly wished we could just go back to the
hotel. I don't care about shopping when I'm home, much
less while I'm here. Because I've seen the marketplaces
we've passed day after day, I have no intention of eating
anything from the roadside vendors. Any souvenirs I
might be interested in buying I would purchase from the
two men that camp outside our hotel gate every day trying to earn enough money to send their children to
school. Maybe it's just that I'm missing Marilee and processing the "I might never see her again" emotions that
seem to be overwhelming me.

While at the marketplace we actually spent very little time
shopping. Most of us came home with a trinket or two, but we all
walked to the end of the row of vendors, stood on the edge of the
roof of a building overlooking a valley, and took in an unbelievable
sight. For as far as the eye could see, in any direction, were tents
and the ruins of buildings where thousands of people live.

Far below us was a muddy river that ran through the valley.
We could see people walking down the steep path to the river to
gather water in buckets. We could also see them wash their clothes
in the same water, along with the dogs and goats that waded in the
water to get a drink or cool off.

From where we stood we were surrounded by evidence that
during the earthquake some of the buildings had literally collapsed
straight down like an accordion. We were standing on top of a
building adjacent to an enormous pile of rubble that had once been
a four-story building. One estimate says 2,200 people are entombed
in that one building alone. Like so many other buildings, there is
not enough money or manpower to dig through the rubble. We
were told that if you were lucky enough to have had a house and a
piece of property prior to the earthquake, it would cost approxi-

mately $3,000 to clear the rubble from your lot in order to be able to begin to rebuild. With record high unemployment rates and the average worker making $4 per day, many lots had still not been cleared.

We finally arrived in front of the presidential palace in late afternoon. Haiti's largest tent city fills the land across from the ruins of the palace. I was surprised to learn that we were going to get out and walk around the area. Pastor Noel is extremely knowledgeable and gave valuable background and insight as we walked around the side of the palace and down the first block. People were beginning to notice the crowd of white people touring the ruins of their capital. I wondered if it bothered them that we were there marveling in the destruction of their homeland. I kept my eyes open, and my travel buddy kept close, as we followed Pastor Noel, hanging on his every word.

Another block down and we were moving farther and farther from our bus, and from our world. It is one thing to experience this poverty from behind the window of the bus. It is quite another to walk right through it. While the day was waning, and we may have been losing some sunlight, I felt a different kind of darkness growing with each step. I wanted to take in all the sights, sounds, and smells, but I didn't want people to think I was staring at them in their plight. There were things that made me long to be a professional photographer, yet I didn't want anyone to feel they were on display. My head spun from the burden God was putting on my heart and the need to find a way to share it.

We got to the end of the next block and instead of turning around and heading back, Pastor Noel turned down the side street. We were deep in the heart of things and far from the security of our bus. Poverty, sick-

ness, sewage, the myriad of smells choked my senses. I
secretly held my breath for a few seconds seeking refuge
for my nose. I feel ashamed to admit that, but I am being
honest.

Just then my travel buddy urged me to step off the
sidewalk and into the street. He pulled me to the side
just in time for me to avoid a large pile of human feces.
Someone had obviously been sick. No one had bothered
to clean it up.

My sandal clad feet stepped off the deep curb and
the sludge running down the street washed over my feet.
I could smell it. I could feel it. I could do nothing about it.
I was on sensory overload. Little did I know then that
God would use even that moment to speak to me.

We turned onto yet another block, which was at
least taking us back in the direction of our bus. This block
had yet another surprise for us. Here, in the middle of
absolute abject poverty, where even a cup of clean drinking water is impossible to find, where half-shredded tents
are the common living quarters, was a car wash. Not an
official building with spinning brushes and all, but five or
six men with buckets and suds washing cars by hand. I
couldn't help but wonder, "Where did the cars come
from?" Or, "How much does a car wash cost in this
neighborhood?" Or even, "Where in the world did you
get the water?" The streets were full of all kinds of unattended sewage, but at least there would be clean cars…

As we got a little farther down the street, another
tent city appeared on our right. Children were peering
out to see the passersby. As with every other child we'd
seen that week, a camera was as much of a draw as candy. Karen and Kate, forever reaching out to the children,
any children, took out their cameras and so it began. One

girl smiled for the camera and then ran over to see herself reflected in the tiny screen on the back. Then another. Then another. Soon we were being followed by some
boys intent on being stars themselves.

As we kept walking, they kept following. I began to
feel a little uneasy. First because they were walking so far
away from their tents. Silly American mother that I am, I
couldn't help but wonder what their mothers would think
of them following the strangers down the block and
around the corner. I quickly realized there might not
even be a mother, and in this place, under these conditions, following the friendly foreigners down the road was
probably the least of their worries. But I was also concerned because their fervor for the camera, or a dollar,
or anything of value we might have was intensifying.

We were nearing a large, very open intersection
when I felt something out of place. I couldn't put my fin-
ger on it right away, but something was different. From
the corner of my eye I noticed a man slumped down on
the sidewalk up ahead and to our right. That was it. He
was alone. I mean, completely alone. In a city where there
are people on top of people on top of people, he sat in
complete obscurity. For several yards to either side of
him was only empty sidewalk. How he seemed to fasci-
nate me. As we got closer I could see clothing that had
not been changed in quite some time, possibly even since
the earthquake. Hints of tan colored shorts hid beneath
layer upon layer of dirt. He sat leaning to the right, his
knees pointing away from us, though his torso was twisted in our direction. He never moved. He never looked
up. I noticed something hanging down but tried not to
stare. I searched for his face, but it was buried. Never did
a muscle flinch, nor was there any sign that he was aware
of the bustling city around him. I looked again to see what

was dangling near the sidewalk. Suddenly it hit me with
the force of a prizefighter's fist. The force of the blow
sent tears to my eyes, though I fought to hold them behind my eyelids. His pants had slipped down below his
thigh. What I saw was him. Totally exposed. I felt as if
somehow I'd violated him by looking. Thoughts whirled
through my brain. As we walked on, the voices around
me seemed so distant. The voice in my head drowned
out all the others. "Why doesn't somebody help him?" I
thought. "Someone should help him cover himself." Then
another voice, a voice from somewhere deep inside me,
spoke and said, "What purpose would that serve, besides
making it easier for you to look at him?" I felt crushed. I
felt convicted. I felt ashamed that I didn't do anything.
And I felt afraid to try.

I walked in such turmoil the rest of the way to the
bus. Pastor Noel continued his role as tour guide, but I
couldn't pay attention. My mind was still reeling. I felt as if
I should go back. I knew I couldn't. I turned back in his direction. "I should do something," I said to myself. "You
can't go back there," I answered. I turned back to our
team.

Boys continued to follow the cameras down the
street. Something bothered me. Maybe it was the way
more and more people seemed to be gathering around
us. Maybe it was the fact that Karen clearly had to keep
the camera strap around her wrist so as not to "lose" it
to an adoring child. Despite the distance we had walked,
despite the fact that we were heading back toward the
bus, my spirit began to stir inside me much in the same
way it had at the light pole.

We crossed the street and my eyes pleaded for
someone to understand what had just hit me. I silently
begged those in my group to acknowledge the assault. No

one did, though Pastor Stan shot me a knowing glance and I sensed he had heard my silent cries.

As we crossed the last intersection in sight of the bus, the ominous feeling inside me grew. More boys had surrounded us. Many of them were bigger than me. Not all of them were smiling. Some of them looked hungry. Some of them looked hollow. The hollow ones felt dangerous. I sensed we needed to stop mingling and get onto the bus. I wondered what precipitated that feeling; something of my own lacking? Or was it the Spirit's leading? A subsequent conversation with Pastor Stan confirmed the latter.

Once inside the bus, the force of the emotional blow I had received earlier could no longer be contained. The dam I had used to hold back the tears burst and I could not stop crying. Lauren sat next to me and caressed my arm gently. She had not seen what I had, but she sensed my need to be comforted. I so appreciated her gentle touch and her kind words. I wanted to tell her everything. I wanted her to know what had just happened. But all I could do was cry.

As we traveled back to our hotel, I sat alone on the bus trying to process my thoughts. I knew I needed to share, but what I needed to share went far beyond cute children. Ironic, isn't it? If an eight-year-old boy was walking the streets naked, we'd probably smile and say, "poor thing." We might even take a National Geographic style picture. But a naked man, that's just not talked about.

Upon returning to the hotel I had no choice but to grab my notebook and try to put into words what God had shown me. This is what I wrote:

I am the invisible man. No one can see me. Not because of any superhuman powers, but from a complete lack of any power at all.

There was a time when that was not so. There was a time, before my world shook beneath me, when the sight of me would send a smile shooting across the face of my wife. I loved the way she looked at me. I was much more handsome when reflected in her eyes.

My children waited every day to see me coming through the big steel gate that leads into our home, our own little world. Both of them would rush toward me to see who could hug me first. Sometimes when I held my daughter I'd notice her staring at my face. I think she was trying to see her own reflection in my eyes.

Peace filled our home each night as the children slept. My beauty and I embraced, and I breathed in the scent of her as we, too, succumbed to sleep.

But that is not the smell that now permeates my nostrils each day. And no longer do the children run to me. The rubble inside the huge steel gate holds them captive and I've not enough money to pay the ransom.

For so long after that horrible day I sat and wished I were invisible. It seems now that I've gotten my wish. I cannot remember the last time I felt a human touch. I hear thousands of voices all around me and yet not one of them is speaking to me. Hundreds of eyes are diverted each day as people pass by and turn away at the sight of me. You passed right by me today, but did not see me. Or if you did, you pretended to look across the street or chose to talk instead to the one next to you meant to protect you from the invisible ones like me.

Tonight you will carefully wash the mud and filth off your feet. That same flow will be my pillow. Too many nights of mud and hunger. I lie here totally, completely exposed. Such exposure normally reserved for the shower, or the bedroom if you still have one.

But I don't blame you. I am so pathetic, and so wracked with pain, that even my mind has decided to leave me. Why should I expect *you* to stay?

I hear people talking to the homeless children all the time. They are clearly easier to see than me. They tell the children there is a God that loves them. They say no matter what, no matter where, even in the dark and dangerous tent city, God is always with them and will watch over them. I guess He is terribly busy with the children just now, because I am completely alone. There was a time when I thought God was all-seeing, but now I have to wonder, for it seems I am invisible to Him, too.

For months before I went to Haiti I consistently prayed the words of a popular song, "Father, break my heart with what breaks yours." That week, that very day, He answered my prayer. Now I wonder, "Can I handle it?"

I Saw God Today

That last day in Haiti was the hardest. There is so much need. Evidence of the need attacked every sense in our bodies: what we saw, what we heard, what we smelled…

But there was also the unmistakable evidence of the Spirit of the Lord moving there. Each day we were encouraged to define our "God moments," or how we saw God at work that day. In a place where the need can be overwhelming, it is important to remember that God is there. God is actively pursuing their hearts. God is love. And God is victorious!

Here are some of the thoughts I held in my heart that week.

I Saw God today… in the face of a man we nicknamed "Rambo" gently holding a young baby boy in his arms.

I saw God today... in the faithful women who spend day after day hand washing clothes for 150 children, their love-filled devotion lived out with plastic tubs and soap suds.

I saw God today... in the heart of a woman who came to Haiti over 30 years ago and stayed to minister to those whom few others could reach.

I saw God today... in a missionary pastor who travels from country to country, not in elegant resorts, but in the world's most needy places–so he can help others experience and understand the challenges, victories, and significance of short-term missions.

I saw God today in the smiles and laughter of children playing in the safety of the orphanage walls.

I saw God today... as some of the men of our group intentionally put themselves between us and an angry mob; one of whom determined that, if need be, he would sacrifice his safety for ours.

I saw God today... as He intervened so that man's sacrifice was not needed.

And I saw God today... as I looked in the mirror and realized I've been forever changed.

Time to Go Home

Suitcase in hand, I look out from this balcony one last time. Just six days ago I stood in this same spot and saw only strangers in a strange land. Now I see people. People in great need; in a land of great need. People I long to reach.

I stand here, a person changed, and hopefully a catalyst of change for others. I know I made a difference this week. But I also know there is so much more to be done. My heart feels like it's being torn in two. I miss my family deeply. I am more tired than I can ever remember being. One last plane ride stands between me and my husband who I know will be waiting for me at the baggage claim. I long to collapse into his waiting arms and hold him forever.

At the same time I don't want to leave. Actually, that's not exactly true. I need to go. I need to breathe and renew my strength. I need to allow my senses and emotions to breathe as well. But I also need to come back, and wonder how long it will be before I can return. Good-bye, dear Haiti.

In the days and weeks since our trip, I have struggled to leave that place. Haiti. My heart cries out for you daily. For the girls on the veranda, for the invisible man on the sidewalk, for the 1.3 million people still living–no, barely existing–in tents, for those whom God would have me love. "Haiti, Oh My Haiti." Now I understand.

The End . . . for now.

But you will receive power when the Holy Spirit comes on you, and you will be my witnesses in Jerusalem, and in all Judea and Samaria, and to the ends of the earth.

Acts 1:8 NIV

AFTERWORD

"In Jerusalem, and in all Judea and Samaria, and to the ends of the earth," God is calling us to reach out to everyone we encounter. We must seek out opportunities to reach those with whom we come in contact in our everyday lives.

Some will engage in His mission more deeply in their immediate communities, such as at soup kitchens or shelters or after-school outreach programs.

Some will engage in His mission more deeply by going farther from home such as Joplin, Missouri, after the tornadoes, or the hurricanes in the gulf coast; to the desperately poor in the Appalachian Mountains or on Native American reservations.

Others will engage in His mission more deeply in foreign countries, working in places like orphanages, clinics, or feeding programs.

Still others will engage in His mission more deeply by generously giving of their financial resources, partnering with brothers and sisters in Christ, enabling them to live out their call.

All of these are equally crucial to the Lord's call to us in Acts. We must each be faithful to that which God is calling us to do.

I realize this can be daunting to some, especially the first time you reach out in unfamiliar places. But like my friend Guy, God will use and transform you. In what has been called The Great Commission in Matthew 28, God not only tells us to go, he promises us *"... surely I am with you always..."* We do not go alone. Nor, as the quote from Acts above tells us, do we go in our own power.

If you feel compelled to help someone in your own town, neighborhood, church, or even family, do so! Reach out with your whole heart and bring His love to them. Feed them, clothe them, visit them; whatever you feel the Lord is calling you to do, do it faithfully. Without you, local missions could not survive.

If you feel compelled to go to a foreign land, then go! You will never regret it and God will meet you there and give you the privilege of helping change lives for Him. Without the extra help, foreign missionaries could not survive.

If you feel compelled to give, then give! Give with all your heart! God will take your generous gifts and use them to provide for the needs of the missionaries and those they care for. Without financial giving missions could not survive.

We are ALL called to be part of His mission. Of that I'm sure. We must all be faithful to live out that call in whichever way He asks us to. We must also respectfully allow others to do the same. Be the hands. Be the feet. Be the wallet! Just BE something, and together, we will be the body of Christ.

INTRODUCING THE AUTHOR

Natalie Ryan is the founder and executive director of Hearts In Action, Inc., a nonprofit organization dedicated to serving children and their caretakers in the most marginalized areas of the world. In that role she was pivotal in the planning and creation of the Home of Hope Orphanage in Sierra Leone. She is also a successful businesswoman, having worked as an award-winning associate, district sales coordinator, and state train-ing coordinator with Aflac insurance company.

Natalie is first and foremost a woman of faith. Her deep commitment to those in need is deeply rooted in her commitment to Christ as the Lord and center of her life. This journey of faith has been punctuated by times of trial and testing, but her life's testimo-ny is one that declares that God is ever faithful.

Natalie finds joy in her role of wife and mother of three sons. This November, Natalie and her husband celebrated their thirty-first anniversary. They live in Rhode Island and are active members of Christ the King Church.

CONTACTING THE AUTHOR

Natalie Ryan is available for speaking engagements at any of the following events:

- Churches and regional conferences
- Youth Group events
- Women's Retreats
- Christian School Missions Projects
- Short-term Missions trips for youth and/or adults
- Book signings
- Fundraising partnerships for schools/churches/missions teams
- Other events considered as schedule permits

For more information please contact:

Dr. Kevin Ryan, President

Hearts In Action, Inc.

PO Box 164

Hopkinton, RI 02833

hearts_in_action@yahoo.com